BROTHER, I HAVE COME TO ARREST YOU

THE TRUE STORY OF ERITREA'S UNLIKELY CHRISTIAN REVOLUTIONARY

DR BERHANE ASMELASH

WITH ANDREW BOYD
AND KENNETH HARROD

Brother, I Have Come to Arrest You

First published in Great Britain in 2024 by
Release International. PO Box 54, Orpington,
United Kingdom BR5 4RT
www.releaseinternational.org
Telephone: +00 44 (0)1689 823491

Copyright © 2024 Release International

Edited by Laura Hayes

The moral right of Dr Berhane Asmelash to be identified as the author of this work has been asserted in accordance with the Copyright, Designs and Patents Act of 1988.

All rights reserved. No part of this work may be reproduced, stored in an information retrieval system (other than for purposes of review) or transmitted in any form or by any means, electronic, mechanical, photocopying, recording or otherwise, without the express permission of the publisher. Any person who does any unauthorised act in relation to this publication may be liable to criminal prosecution and civil claims for damages.

This book is sold subject to the condition that it shall not, by way of trade or otherwise, be lent, resold, hired out, or otherwise circulated without the publisher's prior consent in any form of binding or cover other than that in which it is published and without a similar condition including this condition being imposed on the subsequent purchaser.

A CIP Catalogue of this book is available
from the British Library

ISBN 978-0-95-596937-9 (Paperback)

Cover and layout design by Chandler Book Design
www.chandlerbookdesign.com

Printed in Great Britain by
Short Run Press Ltd.

CONTENTS

	Foreword	1
	Eritrea: the 'North Korea of Africa'	3
	Eritrea Timeline	4
	What the world is saying about Eritrea	6
	Prologue: It begins…	8
1.	Her name meant praise	12
2.	'Let us sing. We will be satisfied tomorrow'	17
3.	An unlikely revolutionary	26
4.	Rumblings of war	29
5.	'Execute the spies'	34
6.	'Brother, I have come to arrest you'	42
7.	The gentle assassin	46
8.	The furious commando	54
9.	News of my execution	59
10.	Opposition and opportunity	63
11.	An overwhelming sense of unease	69
12.	'You will never see your mother again'	77
13.	From kindness to cruelty	81
14.	Asmara under fire	84
15.	Along came Alem	90

16.	Under God's curse?	95
17.	Changing lives	101
18.	Gathering storm clouds	108
19.	Called out and called up	115
20.	Release Eritrea	120
21.	Backlash	124
22.	Helen Berhane	130
23.	Release International	137
24.	Decision Time	144
25.	Twen Theodros	146
26.	Delivered to our enemies	151
27.	Suffering servants	158
28.	Carrying the cross	163
29.	Speaking truth to power	168
30.	Obey the call	171
	Appendix: Twen's story	175
	Aster's Story	185
	Testimonials	187

FOREWORD

Dr Berhane Asmelash is a remarkable man. He remains a humble, clear-thinking servant of Christ and of Christ's suffering people. And it is a great privilege to call him a friend.

His humility and his devotion to Christ, to the gospel and to those who suffer for that gospel shine through in what you are about to read, as he shares his life story and the ministry to which the Lord has called him. Particularly powerful, in this regard, are those times when you see him really feeling – or, at least, identifying with – the pain of those who continue to suffer for their faith.

This book really divides into two parts. In the first part we get to know Berhane himself: his childhood, his upbringing and how he came to faith in the Lord Jesus Christ. We also encounter his own suffering for Christ. This was back in the day when his homeland of Eritrea was part of Ethiopia. The persecution Berhane experienced himself was from the then Marxist regime in Ethiopia.

But then in the second half of the book we follow Berhane's story after Eritrea gained its independence in the 1990s. In particular, we read of the role and calling he has come to fulfil since relocating to the UK: namely, in supporting Christians who have suffered severe, barbaric persecution for their allegiance to Christ and the gospel, at the hands of the Eritrean authorities.

Like Richard Wurmbrand, the Romanian pastor whose life and testimony inspired the founding of Release International, Berhane is someone who has seen both sides of the coin, as it were: that is, someone who has suffered severe persecution himself and who is now working tirelessly to care for and to provide for those who suffer persecution today.

His thoughtful biblical reflection on persecution challenges anything that would smack of superficial Christianity, particularly in those of us blessed to live relatively comfortable lives while professing to be followers of Jesus. But those reflections on persecution also challenge modern-day perversions of Christianity which tell us that the object or result of faith is to live a life of worldly blessing, be that of health or material wealth. The notion of the Christian denying self and taking up his or her cross is a theme that runs through this moving book, whether Berhane is referring to his own experiences, or those of other bold and faithful Christians he has come into contact with.

Towards the end of the book he writes, 'When I decided to follow Jesus Christ, I gave my life to die. And that means being willing to live for Him as well as die for Him. It means dying to my own plans and living for His.'

In many ways that is an apt summary of the spirit that pervades this book.

It is a matter of great pleasure and satisfaction that Release International is able to publish this powerful, moving account. The vast majority of us who read it are unlikely to face the kind of traumatic, painful suffering of the people we encounter as we read. But we can join Berhane in identifying with those who are at the sharp end when it comes to experiencing the world's hatred of Christ – always being mindful of the Apostle Paul's declaration that in the Body of Christ 'if one member suffers, all suffer together' (1 Corinthians 12:26).

Paul Robinson, *CEO Release International*

ERITREA: THE 'NORTH KOREA OF AFRICA'

Eritrea has been described as 'the North Korea of Africa' and 'Africa's largest prison'.

This strip of Red Sea coast in the horn of Africa is about the size of England. It is home to six million people and is divided mainly between Christians and Muslims. It has been ruled since 1993 by a communist-inspired single-party state that represses all opposition. And after unbroken decades in power, Eritrea remains one of the poorest countries in the world.

The government has imprisoned thousands of political activists and attempts to repress and control the church. Most Christians are members of the Eritrean Orthodox Church. The government removed its patriarch Abune Antonios in 2005 for resisting state control.

Evangelical and Pentecostal Christians, whose churches have been forced to close, but who continue to meet in secret, are routinely arrested and imprisoned. They are held indefinitely without trial and face beating and torture by security forces to force them to renounce their faith.

According to the United Nations more than half a million Eritreans have fled the country, mainly to escape conscription, which is both mandatory and indefinite. Many former Christian prisoners have joined the refugees.

ERITREA TIMELINE

1869	Eritrea is established as an Italian colony and wholly occupied by 1889.
1941	World War II. British forces occupy Eritrea during their campaign against the Italians.
1952	Eritrea is federated with Ethiopia, despite opposition from the Eritrean Assembly.
1961	The Marxist-Leninist Eritrean Liberation Front (ELF) is formed to fight a guerrilla war for independence, drawing much of its support from the Muslim population.
1962	The Eritrean government is dissolved in 1962, ending the nation's autonomous status and leading to a 30-year struggle for independence from Ethiopia.
1970	The Eritrean People's Liberation Front (EPLF) is formed, drawing support from the Christian population and uniting other armed groups.
	The relationship between the ELF and the EPLF begins to deteriorate in the mid-1970s, before escalating into open warfare. The EPLF attacks the ELF's headquarters in Nakfa, and after a six-month battle drives out the ELF.

1974	Ethiopian emperor Haile Selassie is overthrown in a military coup.
1981	The EPLF launches a major offensive against the ELF, and by the end of the year, has captured most areas under ELF control.
1991	The EPLF takes Asmara, the capital of Eritrea.
1993	Eritreans vote overwhelmingly in a referendum for independence from Ethiopia. Isaias Afwerki becomes the country's first president.
	Afwerki, a Marxist-Leninist, is a founding member of the EPLF, which he transforms into the People's Front for Democracy and Justice. He promises multi-party elections, then suspends the constitution, ruling Eritrea as the authoritarian head of a single-party state.
1998–2000	Eritrea goes to war with Ethiopia over a border dispute. Described as one of the deadliest conflicts in Africa, it leads to some 80,000 deaths and economic devastation.
2001	The Eritrean government cracks down on political dissent and independent media, resulting in the closure of private newspapers and the arrest of government critics.
2002	The Eritrean government passes a law recognising only four religious denominations: Eritrean Orthodox, Roman Catholic, Lutheran and Sunni Islam. Repression of minority religions follows, including Evangelicals and Pentecostals.
2018	Eritrea and Ethiopia sign a peace deal ending decades of hostility and border disputes.
2020	Eritrea enters the conflict in Tigray, Ethiopia, siding with the Ethiopian government against the rebels. Reports follow of Eritrean troops committing atrocities against civilians.

WHAT THE WORLD IS SAYING ABOUT ERITREA

United Nations:

The UN Commission of Inquiry on Human Rights in Eritrea has accused the government of committing crimes against humanity, including torture, rape, and murder.

'The Special Rapporteur continues to receive reports of the detention of large numbers of people for their actual or perceived religious beliefs, in particular members of unregistered churches, including the Evangelical Church, the Full Gospel Church, the Seventh Day Adventist Church, the Jehovah's Witnesses, the Pentecostal Church, and other Protestant denominations.

'Reports indicate that those detained are subjected to severe torture and other cruel, inhuman or degrading treatment or punishment, resulting in a number of deaths in custody.'

– *Report of the Special Rapporteur on human rights in Eritrea.*

US State Department:

The US State Department has designated Eritrea as a 'country of particular concern' for religious freedom violations.

'Religious detainees, including Jehovah's Witnesses and Pentecostals, continued to be among [those] incarcerated for their beliefs, many of whom have been detained without charge or trial for over a decade.' – *International Religious Freedom Report.*

United States Commission on International Religious Freedom (USCIRF):

'USCIRF continues to receive reports of the Eritrean government's mistreatment and imprisonment of members of unrecognized religious groups. For example… 70 evangelical Christians were arrested in Asmara and held incommunicado in Mai Serwa Prison. Reports indicate that they were subjected to torture and other forms of abuse.

– *USCIRF Annual Report: Eritrea.*

Release International:

Release International and Open Doors have both named Eritrea as a country of concern. Eritrea is listed in Release International's annual *Persecution Trends* report, and the country has risen to number 4 on the Open Doors *World Watch List*.

Reports by Release International state: 'The Christian population in Eritrea is being persistently targeted by the authorities for its faith. Christian detainees face horrific conditions, with reports of torture, malnutrition and disease.

'Eritrea is one of the most repressive regimes in the world, where Christians are routinely rounded up and put in shipping containers in the scorching heat, where temperatures reach up to 40C. They are often left to die or killed outright.'

Many Christians have fled. Release International is supporting Christian refugees in camps in neighbouring countries, through its partner organisation, Release Eritrea.

Release Eritrea's co-founder Dr Berhane Asmelash was accused of being an anti-revolutionary and imprisoned. The justification given was his alleged opposition to the communist government of Ethiopia. He considers his faith to be the main reason for his arrest. He tells his story, along with that of his nation's persecuted Christians in these pages.

PROLOGUE: IT BEGINS...

Wenjel Mirmera Investigation Centre, Asmara. April 1980.

Wenjel Mirmera Prison was constructed by the Italians during the Second World War, and judging by the depth of the dust, had probably not been cleaned since. Two muscular soldiers grabbed me by my skinny biceps and hauled me effortlessly down the long, narrow corridor. The taller of the two, a lieutenant, was well built. His colleague, a sergeant, was shorter, paler and leaner, but also boasted muscles honed by military service. As for me, I was 23 and as scrawny as a chicken. My two beefy captors had little trouble propelling me along the corridor towards the interrogation room.

The place of my torture was five metres by four. The soldiers dumped me in the dust and informed me they would get whatever they wanted out of me with a stick. Even in the poor light, I could make out that stick propped up in the corner, along with whips and a machine sprouting electrodes. But my eyes were drawn to a ditch in the floor, with steps leading down to it.

And then I realised we were not alone. The room had two other occupants, both men. One was subdued and sitting in silence, the other unconscious. Presumably recent clients of my interrogators.

I didn't fear the torture because I simply didn't believe it would happen. I was convinced God would intervene to prevent it. As a new Christian, I had read the New Testament story of how Peter had escaped from prison. Perhaps God would open my prison doors, too. But if the torture did come, then I knew God would give me the grace to withstand it.

Whatever may follow, I was certain God would deliver me from my captors' hands – and I told them so. The two soldiers found that amusing. 'There is no God,' they laughed. What was abundantly evident though were the whip, that stick, and the machine with electrodes. 'Tell us everything you know,' they said, 'otherwise this stick will pull up everything.'

I began to pray and to worship. I was thanking Jesus. It kept the fear from rising.

My interrogators cursed me, slapped me, cuffed my hands and blindfolded me with a dirty handkerchief, pulling it tight. I couldn't see a thing. All the while I continued to pray, blocking their steady stream of curses from my mind. As long as I could ignore their words, perhaps I could keep fighting off the fear. I was praising Jesus out loud.

'Quiet! Shut up!' they yelled, forcing me to sit.

They crammed a log beneath my knees and tied my hands beneath it and in front of me, so the log bore down on my forearms. Then they lifted me over the ditch in the floor and placed the ends of the log either side of the trench to take my weight. They suspended me there, leaving me swinging head-first, upside down in the ditch, with the weight of my entire body bearing on my knees, stemming the flow of blood.

One of my captors stepped down into the ditch beside me and gripped my head and shoulders to keep me still. That was the cue for the muscular lieutenant to begin hitting my bare feet with that stick. Over and over. They called him the Doctor, because he was an expert in torture. The pain was terrible.

My wrists were cuffed so tightly that my right hand had already gone numb. Yet still, I was waiting for a miracle.

On and on it went, for ten minutes, 15. 'You have to talk! You support the rebels. You are a spy! You are working for the Eritrean People's Liberation Front! We know everything about you!' But they knew nothing. And still I wondered, when was God going to step in and stop this? I kept on praying, while they kept on yelling at me to shut up.

But how could I be silent? The torture was designed to place the whole weight of your body beneath your knees. That pressure stops the blood. And the handcuffs were so tight that they damaged the nerves on my right hand along the thumb. They hit me so many times on my bare feet with a stick that I lost count. Each blow was like hot water being poured over my feet, until it felt as though my feet were being burned in the fire.

But then I had a clear picture. I saw Jesus on the cross, enduring the slow, agonizing death of crucifixion. Surely, He had carried my sufferings. So why was God permitting this? In a loud voice I cried, 'Jesus, you suffered for me. Why would you allow this?'

And in the middle of that pain came uncontrollable joy.

God's peace. My own pain was becoming the pain of Christ. Instead of my pain, I began to feel His. My own pain was so tiny, and His was so great. I started thanking Jesus for what he had suffered for me. My heart was filled with the Holy Spirit. And through it all, came one thing clearly. The Apostle Paul says we have the treasure of the gospel in 'jars of clay' that God may show that the mighty power at work in us is from Him.

And as I meditated on that, even as they continued to beat me, I felt the power of God within. Even while enduring torture, I was overwhelmed with joy.

God *had* intervened. I had experienced His grace. And it had not come cheap. Despite the pain, I had learned to praise Him. Yes, there was torment, but even in that disappointment

I could see God's grace. Hanging upside down from that log, my head in a ditch, my feet exploding with fire, I experienced a love and a joy that I cannot describe. Like Paul, I found His grace was sufficient for me. I had learned what grace means. And from that moment on, I knew God's grace would always be with me and that would never change. To be overwhelmed with joy is to forget about the suffering of our bodies. Truly, God had intervened. And then I fell quiet.

They threw me back into my prison cell, shared with 45 others, crammed together in the stifling heat, with barely an inch to lie down to sleep. I looked around. Every prisoner had been tortured like me. Many were bandaged and had come off far worse. Most were clad only in their underwear and each was glistening with sweat. A single, stinking toilet served us all. There were criminals of every kind in that cell. Some were about to face execution.

And as I looked around, I realised with astonishment what God's purpose was for me.

And so it began.

1

HER NAME MEANT PRAISE

The Apostle Paul wrote to his younger friend, Pastor Timothy: 'I am reminded of your sincere faith, a faith that dwelt first in your grandmother Lois and your mother Eunice and now, I am sure, dwells in you as well.' (2 Timothy 1:5; ESV).

I can relate to that. I am thankful to God for my grandparents because they contributed so much to who I am today.

Both sets of grandparents were brought up in the Orthodox Church, but my grandmother on my mother's side, Ymesgen, was raised by Swedish missionaries from the age of five.

Ymesgen had a bone infection in her leg. There were no antibiotics in those days. Her parents brought her to the Lutheran missionaries for treatment, and they took her on to a clinic, some 20 miles from home. The Swedish Christians took good care of her and they raised her separately; and Ymesgen ended up living with those missionaries for 11 years. Over that time, they taught her how to read and write.

Ymesgen had five sisters. The family was all girls. When my great grandfather's first wife died, he remarried and they had two brothers.

Ymesgen was just 16 when she married my grandfather, Welde Gabir, a tall, smart, gentle man who'd converted to the Lutheran faith after hearing the gospel and studying the Scriptures. They lived together in the village of Tala, around

20 miles southwest of Asmara, where they farmed wheat, sorghum and beans, and kept livestock, including bees. They planted cotton and made their own cloth, woven into traditional garments known as *gabi*. These were white, thick for the rainy season, and thin for the summer. The hems were dyed in traditional patterns of red, green, blue and purple.

Along with weaving and beekeeping, Ymesgen and Welde opened a school, offering literacy classes for adults and older children. The Lutheran missionaries tried to pay my grandfather for his services, but he refused, quoting the Scriptures that say as we have freely received, so should we freely give.

Over the years they taught many students. One went on to become a journalist and prominent opposition figure. Weldab Weldemariam was an outspoken critic of the king. And that almost cost him his life. Many times, the authorities tried to assassinate him, until Weldab eventually fled to Egypt and joined the EPLF opposition. Although he was a Christian opposed to violence and refused to take up a gun himself, Weldab supported the resistance, believing the only way to achieve freedom for his country was through revolution.

Grandpa and Grandma were always busy. Their home was often filled with guests – mainly newly converted Christians. They supported orphans and were actively involved in mission work, preaching and teaching in the village.

Lutherans were not always popular, especially among the majority Orthodox community. My grandmother's sister, Hiryti had an early taste of persecution after her husband died.

The Orthodox villagers refused to allow his body to be buried in the cemetery. Hiryti had to inter her husband herself in their own courtyard. People in the village were hoping she would abandon her faith, but Hiryti was a strong woman who remained faithful to Christ.

There was persecution on my father's side of the family, too. My grandfather, Tesfa Mariam converted to the Lutheran faith after he was married. His father promptly disowned him, and his wife, Mamet, said she would divorce him unless he returned to the Orthodox Church. Tesfa called her bluff and told her to go ahead. But knowing my grandfather was a stubborn man unlikely to change his mind, she remained.

Tesfa was a straight talker with a reputation for being blunt, while Mamet was respected in the village for her kindness.

The persecution didn't let up. The authorities packed my grandfather off to prison for abandoning his Orthodox faith. By now Mamet was pregnant. She gave birth shortly after Tesfa was released. They named their baby Asmelash. It means 'Restorer', 'Redeemer' – one who returns something taken by force. That child became my father.

On the other side of the family, my mother Tsedal had been taught to read and write when she was just six. Her first reading book was the New Testament. She memorised the chapters, the genealogy of Jesus and large parts of the Apostle Paul's letters. And when the Old Testament became available in her language, she read that, too.

Inevitably, the persecution grew. The whole family came under pressure from villagers who were members of the Orthodox Church. Protestant Evangelicals were a small minority. Wherever my grandparents went people would make fun of them. They insulted us for not venerating Mary or the saints. But my grandparents continued to show love to the villagers and eventually won them over. They had a daughter who died young and was buried at their farm. But the villagers allowed my grandfather to move the body and give her a proper burial.

At this time the Italians were the occupying power in the country. They intended to keep the Eritreans firmly under their thumb. And that meant preventing them from learning to read and write. But my grandfather continued to teach literacy in secret by writing in the sand. Teaching had been driven underground – a foreshadow of what was to come for Christians under the Communists.

My mother Tsedal grew up to hard work and the sound of singing. She would get up at four every morning to grind wheat, sorghum, and grains on a stony mill; to bake, cook and tend the crops and creatures on the family farm. The house was often filled with singing, and she fondly recalled sitting next to her father as he read from God's word. The family had fellowship with other Protestants, often travelling to different villages to meet in their homes. Eventually my mother was sent to another village, Tseazega, to study with the missionaries.

It was through church that Tsedal met my father Asmelash, although they were living some 30 miles apart. Theirs was an arranged marriage. Tsedal was 15, while Asmelash was 22. They married in 1933. Two years later, the Italians conscripted Asmelash into their army. It almost got him killed – by the British.

To understand why the British were involved, we need to go back to the late 19th century and the scramble for Africa by the colonial powers. In 1869, the Italians grabbed a slice of land on the Red Sea coast and named it Italian Eritrea. By 1890, they declared it a colony. Their ambition was to penetrate deeper into Abyssinia (later known as Ethiopia) but they were held at bay by tough and determined opposition. Italy was forced to put its expansion plans on hold until the years preceding World War II.

Under delusions of reviving the Roman Empire, the Italian fascist dictator Mussolini recruited soldiers from Eritrea for a second great push into the region. It was then they conscripted my father. Pitting a modern army with machine guns against spears they went on to conquer Ethiopia.

Six years later in 1941, my father was captured by the British when the Allies invaded Ethiopia to drive out the Italians. They sent my father to prison, where rumours were circulating that the prisoners were to be executed in the morning. My father managed to cut through the barbed wire fence and make his escape.

He walked all the way back to Eritrea – a journey which took him three weeks. He survived by selling his military fatigues and buying farmer's clothing. And everywhere he went, he bought eggs in one village and sold them in another. Eventually, he found his way home to his wife, Tsedal.

Although their first son died at the age of three, they eventually had seven other children. I was the sixth. Tsedal gave birth to me in September 1956 in the village of Himbrti, to the west of the capital, Asmara.

My earliest memory was at the age of four. My sister Abeba was getting married and they had woven purple flowers in her hair.

I slept in the same bed as my paternal grandmother, Mamet, on a raised plinth of stones, smoothed over with mud mixed with animal dung, and then covered with animal hide. We snuggled together beneath a home-made quilt. Mamet was small and with skin so pale that some thought she must be Italian. She was in her 70s when she died. The family surrounded her bed and she smiled at them as she breathed her last. My mother said Mamet had smiled because she was a godly woman.

My maternal grandfather died at the age of 90, in 1972 from gangrene of the foot. And my grandmother died at the age of 96. I used to visit them often. I fondly recall my grandmother's immaculate handwriting and how she used to sing for me, both in Amharic and Swedish. She was clear-headed until the day she died. My godly grandparents helped shaped the man I was to become.

2

'LET US SING. WE WILL BE SATISFIED TOMORROW'

My mother Tsedal was tall, kind and generous. She was forever sharing our food with our poorer neighbours in Himbrti, and in Asmara who would smell the cooking and come over. She gave everything away. She was always helping others less well off than us, although we were quite poor ourselves.

Our Lutheran church was nearby. It was red stone, with a grey corrugated iron roof with a cross on top. The church would hold about 80 people. It was a happy place, where everybody knew everyone else. Life was a rhythm of church and playing with the animals, though some of that livestock would play rough. I remember taking a pee outside my house when a goat came up from behind and butted me. I howled. I was absolutely soaked and went running to mother.

My father seldom lived with us during my early childhood. He was a lineman, connecting telephone wires from town to town. He was constantly travelling, spanning out from Asmara 200 miles to connect Eritrea to Ethiopia. He was often away for years at a time. One day a lady came to our house, looked at me and asked: 'Do you know your father?' I had to say no. My mother decided to do something about that, so we moved to a town called Keren so we could be with my father.

To get there we had to walk for three hours before taking a train. It was the first time I'd even seen a train – let alone travelled on one. I was so excited! The carriages were green, the diesel engine was white, and it felt like riding on a giant caterpillar! We trickled through the countryside for about four hours, through tunnels and past mountains. And when we got to Keren my aunt and father were waiting for us in the station. I was so excited, I couldn't wait to open the door. I climbed out of the carriage window to greet them.

Keren means mountain, and the town was surrounded by mountains; the buildings were sandy white beneath the sun, and clean and beautifully constructed in the Italianate style. Our garden had a lime tree and there were fruit trees everywhere – mango, oranges and guava. I would run around in my bare feet in my black jumper and shorts.

By now, my baby teeth were working loose and my father asked me if I wanted him to pull them out. I refused, but then he promised to buy me my first pair of shoes, so out they came. Our time together was short-lived.

For the first year we lived in the telecommunications building where they accommodated their workers. But before long, my father got transferred to Massawa and we became homeless. Someone kindly gave us a small round house. It had an earth floor but no roof. So my brothers Bahta and Tadesse, who were now in their early teens, covered the roof with straw. It was always leaking and had to be repaired. I told my mother: 'Our house is like my trousers – full of patches!' She laughed. She was pregnant at the time with my younger sister. Although my elder sister was already married, there were still six of us crammed into that dilapidated hut.

Even with all these children, my mother was determined to send us to school. Schooling was a rarity in those days. Most families held on to their children to help run their farms. But my mother was determined not to let poverty stand in the way of our education. The school in the village only went up to the fourth grade, so my mother sent my eldest sister to the city to continue her studies.

My first school in Keren was run by Methodists. There was a good deal of Bible study and singing:

> *'I'll be true, precious Jesus, I'll be true. (2)*
> *There's a race to be run,*
> *there's a victory to be won,*
> *every hour by thy power,*
> *I'll be true.'*

The school was part of the 'Methodist holiness' movement and very severe. It had a strict dress code. Women had to wear long dresses and jewellery was forbidden.

During Sunday services people were encouraged to come forward and publicly confess their sins. One boy stood up and confessed to making fun of one of the teachers with a club foot. All the children laughed. Even the teacher with the club foot smiled. But confession could be a serious business. People would confess everything from adultery to drunkenness and often cry while confessing their sins at the service.

One day I was listening to an American radio station and humming along to the country music when a friend at school rebuked me: 'When you go to hell,' he said, 'you'll remember this song.'

'Why should I go to hell?' I asked him.

He said: 'Because you are singing a secular song.'

Fear was constantly lurking in the background. I heard from someone in another town Dekemhare, one missionary would stand on the rooftop on Sundays to look out for anyone sneaking off to go shopping. He would warn them and tell them to publicly confess their sin of not respecting the Sabbath.

Eritreans are usually Christian or Muslim. Most of the Christians are Orthodox, and these Orthodox believers considered any other denomination to be a foreign religion.

The Orthodox children used to pick on us. They teased us, 'You Protestants eat cats and dogs.' And they accused us of becoming Protestants just to get money from the Swedish mission: 'Did the missionaries buy you this shirt and trousers?' I never knew how to handle the bullying.

My mother and father mixed well enough with our Orthodox neighbours. And when they got to know us, they respected us. Few could read and they had little knowledge of the scriptures. Mother would always read to them from the Bible, particularly from Matthew and the Beatitudes. And although many were suspicious of our faith, they appreciated our generosity.

We stayed in Keren for about four years. Life was always hand-to-mouth. My father's salary was never enough. He had to split his wages between providing for us and covering his own expenses whenever he had to move to another town for work. On top of that, my father passed on his salary to a relative to give to us. But the man was an alcoholic and drank my father's earnings away.

As a family we learned to overcome hunger by singing and praying. I recall my brother Bahta coming to our house with his friend Sultan. But we had no food to offer our guest. So Bahta took Sultan out for a walk and returned a few hours later. Even by then, we hadn't managed to find any food.

Then there was a knock on the door. Bahta said: 'I hope this friend will bring a blessing.' He was right. It was our sister Abeba, who'd come from one of the nearby villages 20 miles away with a basketful of bread. God knew we had nothing in the home. He had provided and we rejoiced! My mother always said: 'Let us sing. We will be satisfied tomorrow.'

My mother knew most of the hymns in the Lutheran hymnbook. Usually, we would start with the first on page one and go page by page each evening. One of the songs was *What a friend we have in Jesus*. We also sang *Abide with me*, carols at

Christmas and other hymns which are popular in the West. We thanked God for each new sunny day in our language, Tigrinya.

In Keren, our town was predominantly Muslim. Muslim and Christian children played together well, but the Muslim parents were not always so keen. One of our neighbours yelled at her son, 'Mohammed! I told you not to play with those Christians!' When my brother put a cross on the top of our house a neighbour threw stones to try to break it. They made their displeasure even more evident by throwing their rubbish in front of the house.

Eventually one of my sisters, Mebrat, got a job with the Middle East General Mission, training as a health care worker. She also worked in the kitchen of the Mission's Bible school. At the same time my mother started doing paid hairdressing at home. My father didn't approve of her working, because of the stigma of poverty. But we were eventually able to move to a cleaner neighbourhood and gradually our family circumstances improved.

Our next home in Keren was a step up. It was still one room but larger. The floor was paved with cement and this one had a corrugated iron roof. However, my mother decided we needed to return to Asmara, to the capital city to find more work. It was 1966.

As a child, I was skinny, weak and sickly. I had problems with my speaking and struggled to say the letter 'r'. Until I was 16, I couldn't even pronounce my name properly. Everybody laughed at me. Inevitably, I was bullied. I started to hate myself and didn't want to go outside. But my mother was always complimenting me; she would say, 'Berhane, you are majestic, like a king!'

A couple of times I almost drowned. When I was about ten, I was playing with my older brother, Bahta, and fell into a pond. I couldn't swim and would have gone under if he hadn't jumped in to save me. Some years later, I was swimming off the beach in the Red Sea and somehow became disorientated. I was heading away from the shore. By the time I heard my friends calling me, I had no energy to swim back. Fortunately, I was able to tiptoe on some coral and keep my head above water long enough for my friends to swim out and rescue me.

My mother never allowed us to use bad language, swear or to fight. She always said, 'You realise that lying and cursing is a sin.' As a youngster I was sin-conscious and often reluctant to join in games with other boys in the neighbourhood. If I heard them curse or swear, I would run home which gave them another opportunity to make fun of me. Not that they needed any further opportunity. In Asmara we were regarded as very provincial and outsiders. The other children would always make fun of my Keren accent and call me names.

What kept me going was that I always achieved good grades in school and was usually top of the class. I passed my general exam in the sixth grade and was assigned to a middle school some six miles from home. It took me an hour to travel each day. School life improved, but the other boys still loved to make fun of me.

The congregation at our Evangelical Lutheran Church was well-to-do. And that was awkward. I always felt the misfit: too poor and too insecure. My trousers were old and shabby and I was the only one who was not properly dressed. I belonged in the slum, not here. I gave up attending when I was around 14. Eventually I took up going to a nearby mission hall run by the Sudna Interior Mission in Asmara. They organised sports events and taught us music, which I enjoyed. My first instrument was a trumpet, which I played for the brass band in the church. *Thine be the glory* was my favourite.

But at the age of 14 in 1970 I became sick again. I was constantly hungry and thirsty and was still struggling to control my bladder – embarrassing for a boy in his teens. My family would scream at me: 'You are grown up! What's the matter with you?' But even when I didn't drink, I still needed to wee.

I started to hate myself. I was sharing a bed with my brother, Bahta, who was five years older than me. One night I wet the bed three times.

By now Bahta was working as a health assistant. He wondered if I had diabetes. To make matters worse, he told me: 'If it *is* diabetes, you'll never be able to eat sugar again.' I was miserable: no bananas, no biscuits, no honey! Bahta brought me tablets from the hospital to test my urine. Green for normal, but if these tablets turned red then I had too much sugar in my urine. Those tablets turned bright red. And sure enough, when I stopped eating sugar my health improved. At that stage I wasn't taking insulin.

The city centre of Asmara was much more interesting than sleepy Keren. It was full of life. Half the people were foreigners. There were tens of thousands of Italians, Arabs and Americans, with big cars and motorbikes. I was amazed how beautiful the city was. There were flowers and toy shops. But we were still poorer than most and our neighbourhood was a slum.

By now, my brother Tadesse was at a Methodist boarding school and Mebrat was studying to be a nursing assistant some 200 miles away. Bahta had joined Mebrat there and my father was still working in Massawa, leaving just three of us and my mother. Inevitably, I was lonely. My two sisters were girls – how could they be my friends? My only friends were my cousins. When they came over, they protected me from the bullying.

Eventually, Mebrat and my father were able to join us in Asmara. By then, I was 17 and my diabetes was getting worse. After three years, I imagined it would be safe to eat sugar again, but it made me very ill. By then I was six feet tall and as thin as a stick. I had turned very pale because my circulation had stopped and I was drinking water by day and night. I could hardly eat. I felt angry towards my family and blamed them for my illness. Photographs show me as sad, angry and unsmiling. It was only when I found Jesus that my smile returned.

Eventually my sister, who was a nursing assistant, took me to hospital to see a diabetes specialist. By then, I wasn't even able to walk properly. My sister had to support me, even for the short distance from the bus stop to the hospital. The doctor winced when I took off my T-shirt. He proclaimed: 'You're nothing but skin and bones.' He was right. I weighed around 34 kg (about five stone, four pounds). The doctor informed me I would have to take insulin. I said I would rather just control my diet, but he said it was too late for that. By now I couldn't even stand the smell of food, and was close to lapsing into ketoacidosis, a life-threatening complication of diabetes.

The next day a friend cycled to a hospital to get some insulin. My sister gave me my first injection – and within hours my appetite returned. By the time I went back to see the doctor I'd put on weight and was able to walk again, even though I was taking only half the recommended dose. When I started taking the full dose, I quickly grew stronger. By now I'd missed months of school, but I managed to catch up and scrape a pass in the end-of-year exam.

Looking back, all these things helped me get closer to God, although at the time I was constantly afraid of death and hell. I had no real grasp of the grace of God. The Bible was read in our house every day and we sang gospel songs every evening, but I had yet to understand the way of salvation. Christianity was just a tradition for me. But later in life I realised that my upbringing was preparing the way for my salvation.

Mother and father worked hard and prayed hard. They showed us by example how to be true followers of Christ; how to be strong in faith even when things work against you, and how to remain faithful.

My father was a great man of God. He would begin each day before breakfast with a time of Scripture-reading and prayer. He would stand at the doorpost at 6am and read out loud as if to an entire congregation. Even our neighbours could hear him.

Then he would go to work. In the evening we had family devotions, where we would read the Scriptures, sing gospel songs and pray before bed. This was our daily routine, and we all took turns reading the Scriptures.

My father never missed church, except for one Sunday when he was sick and the entire congregation came round to our house. My parents were the most respected people in the neighbourhood and our house was always full of guests. Even though we never had much, my mother was always generous. And because of my parents' influence I have always wanted to support the needy.

When my mother died in 1987, I was 31 years old. It was the darkest day of my life and I was depressed for almost a year. By the time my father died at the age of 92 I was living in London. I was unable to return to Eritrea for his funeral because of the risk of arrest. By then I was campaigning for religious freedom, a campaign that had its roots in revolution and drew inspiration from an unlikely hero of the faith.

3

AN UNLIKELY REVOLUTIONARY

When the British kicked the Italians out of Eritrea in 1941, they had no idea what to do with the country. Eritrea was simply an Italian creation. The British suggestion was to split the country between Ethiopia and Sudan. The US took a different view. They wanted Eritrea to be part of Ethiopia, which was a US ally. Finally, the United Nations suggested the world should give Eritrea time to settle its own issue.

The country was to remain in confederation with Ethiopia for ten years to allow it to develop its own parties and political leaders. The nation was ruled by the autocratic emperor Haile Selassie, hailed for resisting Italian oppression and abolishing slavery, but feared for his brutal suppression of political opposition. And the Emperor began to send his assassins to openly murder politicians and journalists who spoke against him. His reach extended to members of parliament. Some fled the country. Then in 1961, Muslims from the lowlands began a military struggle. And the following year, Ethiopia annexed Eritrea by force.

In 1963, I was seven years old when the conflict came to Keren. The Muslim fighters were already among us. The police were sent to fight the freedom fighters, but some police quit their jobs to join them. 31 police officers were ambushed and killed. Their bodies were brought to the police camp, close to where we lived. And their wives were called in to identify their husbands. One of my mother's cousins was a policeman. She took me to see the bodies. That nightmare has never left me.

Students and pupils were caught up in the unrest. And I found myself sucked into the demonstrations in Asmara. When we got out from school, we went to throw stones at the police. We were off school for months on end. The government ordered us to return to our classes or be dismissed. But we watched and waited. And no one was going to school.

By now, my brother Tadesse had joined the Eritrean Liberation Front, along with many university students. There were two groups of freedom fighters. Both groups were essentially nationalists, but the Eritrean Liberation Front (ELF) were more liberal and democratic. The breakaway Eritrean People's Liberation Front (EPLF) were hard-line communists who worshipped Mao and favoured guerrilla warfare. And while the ELF was initially run by Muslims, Christians later began to join.

I would have joined too, but as a diabetic in need of insulin, I knew they would never accept me. At the time, revolution was in the air like a fashion. We simply didn't understand the risks. We had no idea that thousands would perish. My brother was eventually driven out of Eritrea into Sudan, and from there went to Saudi Arabia.

1974 was the year of the military coup. Haile Selassie, the Emperor who had ruled Ethiopia for more than 40 years, was deposed. The year before had seen unrest throughout Ethiopia. Students, civil servants and taxi drivers were out on the streets, demonstrating against the government over the state of the economy and the need for greater democracy. Young people were calling for change, although we had little idea what sort of change was needed. Setting the tone for what was to come, most of the demonstrations were orchestrated by left-wing groups.

That year a man called Richard Wurmbrand came to our city to speak. He shared his story in the Lutheran school hall, from behind a wooden pulpit. This tall, thin man stood there in his grey suit and spoke of the years he spent in prison, and how he was tortured to try to make him renounce his Christian faith, and how he'd withstood, even though it almost cost him his mind. His sufferings were too much for me; I found it too painful to hear.

Many of the young people in the audience were socialists. They thought Wurmbrand had been sent by the West to indoctrinate us. One boy, who'd been raised in our church orphanage, pointedly suggested Wurmbrand should go away and preach to the hippies. Far from being thrown by this, Wurmbrand retorted that the hippies could preach to themselves.

Some of the left-wing students challenged him over his claim to have suffered under the Communists in Romania. He replied: 'Do you want me to take off my shirt and show you the scars on my back?' This unlikely revolutionary was serious about his faith. He described praising God in prison even while the guards mocked him for being crazy. His words stayed in my mind.

He wrote a book called *Tortured for Christ*. When I read his story, I realised how costly it is to be a follower of Jesus Christ. It was my first exposure to suffering. God was preparing my heart for what would follow. Later, when the revolutionary government declared Ethiopia a socialist nation, I remembered everything Richard Wurmbrand had said. But I was not yet a committed Christian, and I kidded myself I would be safe.

4

RUMBLINGS OF WAR

Back then Eritrea was still part of Ethiopia. In September 1974, I was in the main port of Massawa on the Red Sea coast, when I heard over the hotel radio that king Haile Selassie had resigned and the military had taken over. Then the war came even closer to home. From nearby came the rumblings of a tank and the chatter of machine-gun fire.

Nothing was being reported on the news. We had no idea what was happening. But we later heard that Ethiopian security had rounded up villagers, mainly young boys, and executed them. Some had hidden in the village church to try to save themselves. There were also executions in the street of Asmara. I knew one of these young men, Adam, from Sunday school. He could have been only 20. He was picked up from the street and executed. Another neighbour, about 18 or 19 – my age – was sick and had to go to hospital. He was shot dead by snipers from a rooftop. An Ethiopian sniper also killed our neighbour's six-year-old boy, as he was playing in the field. His name was Jonas.

The Eritrean freedom fighters had entered the city and started shooting. So the Ethiopian army was massacring civilians in revenge. Machine guns and tanks were firing from the street close to our house. 'Get under the bed!' my mother urged. My sister and I crammed ourselves beneath the bed's steel frame.

The shooting went on for several hours. After the gunfire died down, I ventured outside.

Three hundred yards away was a soldier with a gun. Stupidly, I wondered what he was doing. He knelt, took aim and fired at me. I heard the high-pitched zing of the bullet as it passed close to my head. I ran for my life. Later we heard that Ethiopian soldiers had killed 84 people in an Orthodox Church just four miles from our house.

My parents both dreamed of an independent Eritrea. And they were supporting my brother who had joined the revolution. But there were two factions who were fighting for independence, and we were split on which to give our backing, the ELF, or the EPLF.

As the killing continued, my parents insisted they would never leave. My father was adamant: 'I will die in my house.' But eventually my parents sent me with two of my sisters to live with an older sister, in a village hopefully beyond the reach of the Ethiopian army. We stayed there for about six weeks, until the killing subsided.

The Ethiopians had declared themselves to be socialists supported by the Soviet Union. This provoked the anger of the USA and prompted President Jimmy Carter to cut off their supply of weapons to the country. Meanwhile, in Eritrea, the freedom fighters were gathering strength, bolstered by increasing numbers of students and support from Iraq and Syria.

Finally, the revolution came to an end in 1991. Eritrean fighters were joined by Ethiopians from the north, who, with the support of the Tigray People's Liberation Front (TPLF), swept into northern Ethiopia and kicked out the Ethiopian soldiers. President Mengistu fled to Zimbabwe and the TPLF set their sights on the Ethiopian capital, Addis Ababa.

In the turmoil of war, any hope of an education was non-existent. Schooling was out for the duration. There were constant riots and demonstrations. Trying to get insulin to manage my diabetes had become a nightmare. I thought if I went into healthcare, at least I could get access to insulin.

Just before I turned 20, I heard about a one-year training course for health assistants. They sent you to a hospital to work in primary care to help nurses. By then I'd given up any notion of going to university as I thought I would struggle to manage my diabetes, so healthcare seemed a good fit. As it turned out, the course was highly competitive: I was one of only 20 to be selected from 700 applicants.

After my year's training I was assigned to work in Adi Keyh, about 70 miles southeast of Asmara. However, the road was blocked by Eritrean freedom fighters, so we were told we would have to wait for a helicopter or small plane to take us there.

As I was out walking, the health manager passed by in his car. He quickly stopped and called me over. He told me we could travel by plane that day, so I should go home and hastily pack a small bag. My mother was out but fortunately my sister was there, so I was able to explain my sudden departure.

I gathered my bags in a great hurry, pulling out books at random to take with me. One was called *Take my life*. I'd never read it. It was time I did.

Together, the manager, two nurses and all the newly trained health assistants boarded a small plane. It took just 15 minutes to fly to Adi Keyh, but the town was being shelled by Eritrean rebels and we had to circle before the pilot judged it safe to land. When we finally touched down, we scrambled into an army truck and were driven to the hospital. There, we turned some empty wards into makeshift bedrooms. I shared a room with two other men.

The town was depressing and the sound of shelling incessant. There was no Protestant church, only a Catholic church and a few Orthodox churches, none of which appealed to me.

I was unhappy. There were more soldiers than civilians in that small town and there was nothing for me and my roommates to do in the evenings, other than visiting local beer shops, where my two friends would drink too much and became disruptive.

There were two nurses in the hospital – sisters, who were Christians – whom I knew from my church back at home. Their names were Hadas and Ethiopia. They invited me to their house for Bible study. Since I was lonely, I gratefully accepted their invitation.

Hadas and Ethiopia were older than me. Hadas worked hard as a nurse and was always smiling. There was something special about them. They were serious about their faith and tried to share it with everyone.

Back in Asmara, as the civil war raged on, Christians from different denominations began to meet to pray for the country, Hadas and Ethiopia among them. Sometimes I played the piano at these gatherings, and perhaps because of that these two nurses assumed I was more committed to the Christian faith than I was at the time. I appreciated their care and respect towards me, and I wanted to know more about their faith.

So I finally got around to reading the book *Take my life*. It questioned whether I'd given every part of my life to God. I knew I hadn't. I had known Jesus from outside, but he was not part of my life. Inside, I was empty.

I knelt by my bedside and invited Jesus into my life. I prayed: 'Dear God, thank you that you love me. I want now to give every part of my life to you, forever.'

Immediately, I felt a load had been taken from me.

My heart had been empty, and now it was filled with God's love. I was filled with joy! Suddenly, I could see God's purpose for my life, and I knew I had much work to do.

I'd placed my life into His hands and began to feel a new sense of security from God. The fear had gone. I was no longer afraid of being arrested or dying.

From that moment, I became fear-free. All that old anxiety had gone, and from that day on, I would never let myself be bullied again. Even when people tried to bully me, instead of blaming them, I became concerned for them, wondering what their problem could be. I no longer cared what people thought.

And all this happened instantly, the moment I accepted Jesus Christ as my saviour. The missionaries had been saying as much for years, but finally I understood. Now I knew. For the first time in my life, I felt a changed person.

As Paul said, 'If anyone is in Christ, he is a new creation. The old is gone, the new has come.' (2 Corinthians 5:17). There had been a clear and instant transformation in my life. Although I had known the scriptures well, now I began to see the Bible in a new light. The Bible became my life, speaking words of life to me each day.

When I told the sisters what had happened, they were thrilled. But my roommates' reaction could not have been more different.

5

'EXECUTE THE SPIES'

When I told my roommates I'd become a Christian, they were angry and disappointed. They thought I would no longer go with them to the beer shop, so they tried to convince me to quit these Bible studies.

One evening, one of them was drunk and turned hostile. He threw water and cold tea at me. He was my age, about 22 but bigger and stronger than me. I saw a knife on the table. He was becoming violent and out of control. So, I went next door to our neighbours', who invited me to stay the night.

But when I was getting ready for bed I had an uneasy feeling that I just couldn't shake off. I was worrying about my roommate, so I rushed back to our house and found him dangling from the doorpost. He had torn his vest into a rope and was hanging there, unconscious.

I managed to tear him down. Thank God, the vest had some give in it, so he was still alive.

I carried him to his bed and stayed with him. After a while, he opened his eyes, looked at me and tried to raise his arm to hit me, but didn't have the strength. I stayed by his bed all night. The next morning I said nothing. He was clearly embarrassed. And that evening I found him kneeling reading my Bible. From then on, he read the Bible every day and stopped drinking. He had become a Christian.

The town of Senafe nearby had been under rebel control, until the army took it back. The town had a clinic, but the rebels had taken everything, even the doors and the windows. Most of the residents had fled. I was sent there with another co-worker.

By now, I was just 22 years old. My colleague was in his late-50s, a huge, talkative man with a big belly and a gap between his front teeth. We were the first to arrive in the town after its recapture. The shops were closed and there was not a scrap of food to be found.

I said, 'God will provide.' My colleague was sarcastic. But at midday, a girl of about seven or eight arrived in a long dress, with a basketful of soft, sour, fermented injera bread. My colleague said, 'It happened just as you said!' I was so happy to see God's provision.

People came to us from outlying villages with illnesses including malaria, typhoid and other infectious diseases. We also had to assist with births – and even dentistry. The work was certainly varied.

But the man I was working with had a reputation for charging for treatment, even though healthcare in Eritrea had always been free. After I helped a woman give birth, my colleague shouted: 'You should have charged that family!' He screamed at me. I was holding a candle at the time. He was searching through the medical equipment, shouting, 'Why did you use a new pair of gloves while you could use old dirty ones?'

In my anger I smashed the candle into the floor. The room was plunged into darkness and I fell into my bed which was next to me. The next morning, I asked a military friend to help me get back to Adi Keyh, which, thankfully, he was able to do.

By 1979, all around the war was raging, with fighter jets, artillery and tanks. The rebels had blocked the road, and one night, when they tried to take the town, thousands of wounded soldiers were brought to the hospital. Adi Keyh was the only place where wounded soldiers could be cared for. My tasks included night duties, issuing medication and giving injections. The fighting nearby brought a constant stream of wounded government soldiers to us.

All we could offer was a single civilian doctor and 100 beds. There were two soldiers to every bed and we filled the corridors and courtyard, working day and night. We had no idea what to do with all these patients who had gunshot wounds and injuries from landmines. We did our best to stem the bleeding. My heart was heavy from seeing so many patients dying.

We knew the freedom fighters were determined to take the town. You could hear automatic weapon fire, bombs and shelling. The battle raged for three days and three nights. The fighting came to within half a mile of us. As bullets zipped around, we didn't know if we would be hit ourselves. Then a bomb from a fighter jet exploded about 100 metres from the hospital, showering us with debris.

The rebels advanced to within 800 yards of the hospital. They blasted us with mortars and pelted us with bullets from their AK47s. They knew they were attacking a hospital, but they didn't care. We were treating soldiers, and as far as they were concerned, we were a target.

It was pitch black, and the wounded were crying and shouting with pain. I had to go to them. But the moment I switched on the lights, the shooting started again. Quickly, I flipped the lights back off. Every morning we would find many dead among the soldiers. There was no one to care for them. Hundreds died in that hospital and hundreds more in the field.

One wounded rebel fighter was mistaken for a government soldier and brought in for treatment. He recognised a nurse and called her over. She swapped his uniform for hospital clothes. Then she and the soldier ran away and joined the fighters. When the government soldiers found out, they wanted to kill us all for assisting him.

They rounded up all the hospital workers and said they intended to execute us. They needed no excuse. Everywhere, they were killing people without reason. They ordered us to stand in front of the hospital, but the top commander intervened. We never thought we would survive the war. We just wanted to do our best until we died. All around, people were falling like leaves and dying with no one to care for them.

And in that place of chaos and slaughter, we stopped thinking about ourselves.

Finally, after about three days, the freedom fighters, who had taken a pounding, retreated. For the next week we were working frantically with many more patients than we could cope with. I was grateful that my assurance as a Christian gave me peace in my heart in the midst of this.

Since I'd become a Christian, I was ready to go anytime, but I knew God had work for me to do. I wanted to help those who were suffering and dying, to ease their pain and dress their wounds. I could see the change I could bring to that person's life. That was the only skill I had, to just stop the pain. I could give them sleep; I could make things better for them. The soldiers I treated went from shouting and screaming to sleeping in peace. And I was thankful to God for this simple skill.

Before long, the Communist cadre in the town sent us a letter – without warning – informing us that we were to be executed. We were accused of being hired by the CIA to infiltrate the army, to spy on the soldiers and persuade them not to fight. Copies of our death notice were posted around the town and sent to the police and health workers.

How do you respond to a sentence of death?

We had no idea. Hadas, a Christian nurse said, 'God will save us. And if He doesn't want to save us, we will die.' So that was that. We were all in agreement and continued to meet for prayer and worship. The next Sunday our numbers had risen from just a handful to 19.

Our group was studying the book of Daniel. We read the story of Shadrach, Meshach and Abednego. These men held on to their belief in God even when threatened with a fiery death. They told the king: 'O Nebuchadnezzar, we have no need to answer you in this matter. If this be so, our God whom we serve is able to deliver us from the burning fiery furnace, and he will deliver us out of your hand, O king. But if not, be it known to you, O king, that we will not serve your gods or worship the golden image that you have set up.' (Daniel 3:16-18).

The story of these faithful, courageous men served as an inspiration for us all. We were filled with encouragement and determined not to abandon our faith. This cadre who was threatening us had a reputation for executing many young people in the area. Yet, despite it all, more and more people started coming to our Sunday Bible studies.

Eventually our accuser was himself accused and arrested. So we brought him food in prison to show our Christian love.

Later, I befriended a man called Hizechael who was a district attorney. I was delighted when he began to show an interest in Christ. I promised I would see him again the next day, but when I went to his house after work, I discovered he'd been arrested. I took a Bible to the prison to give to him but was unable to find out what had happened. Years later I discovered that he, too, had been executed. Such was the fate of many in the town at that time.

Our Bible study group was becoming increasingly active. We were always sharing the gospel with hospital staff, patients, workers in the government offices and civil servants. In this small town everyone seemed to know everyone else. Perhaps not surprisingly, the authorities were less than happy with what we were doing.

There were three reasons for that, and for the ongoing persecution in Eritrea. The communists were atheists and suspicious of Christianity, which they saw as a Western attempt to undermine their revolution. And, like all autocrats, they wanted total control of all of their people, all the time. In Christian terms, what they really wanted was the worship, just like Nebuchadnezzar in the book of Daniel we'd been reading.

There was a wedding on the outskirts of the town. There was no transportation, so we had to walk. But when we reached the checkpoint on the edge of town we were turned away and had to return home. It was late by the time I got back, but before going to bed I decided to spend a while in prayer.

I'd left the door open and shortly I could hear people standing close by. As I looked out, I could see silhouettes of soldiers with guns. I asked who they were, and they shouted back, 'Put on the light, put on your clothes and follow us.' They bundled me out of the house and into a Jeep alongside four armed soldiers. They drove me to the police station and threw me into a cell. I found myself on the floor, with no mattress or blanket.

I spent three nights in that cell, before being taken to a makeshift prison. I still had no idea what crime I was supposed to have committed, but I was filled with faith. There were more than 40 young people in this prison and they were frightened. I realised God was putting me in this place to minister His word, so I began preaching the gospel. I said,' I am here to tell you the good news that Jesus loves you. God is in control.'

They tried to put me right. 'Once you are here you will never get out,' they said. But I knew God had sent me there on assignment.

While I was talking to them, a police officer called me away to an interrogation room. 'Do you know why you have been arrested?' he asked. I said I didn't. 'You were caught trying to flee the town,' he claimed. I asked how that could be true, as I'd been arrested in my house. I explained what had happened and eventually, when they were able to confirm my story, they released me. But later I heard that most of the group I'd preached to in the prison had been executed.

That was a wake-up call to get on and do the work. And I decided to dedicate my life to preaching the gospel, even though it was officially forbidden.

That same week, Solomon Habib, the youth chairman of the local Communist party, came to my house. He was about 21, intelligent and quiet, and a good listener. He gazed around at the Bible verses on my wall, then along my bookshelf. 'Religion is allowed in communist countries such as Russia and China,' he said, adding this warning: 'You are free to believe – as long as you keep it to yourself.'

The implication was clear. A scripture came to mind: 'For me to live is Christ, and to die is gain.' (Philippians 1:21). I told him: 'I don't care whether they allow it or not, I'm ready to die for it.'

Solomon looked stung. When I was later arrested for a second time, others said this communist leader had missed his chance to convert me to being a communist.

There were a number of Communists in the town who had been trained by the former Soviet Union. They knew I was a Christian and repeatedly told me, 'Your Western religion is from America!' They were opposed to anyone speaking about the Bible and about God and, like Solomon, warned me of the consequences of doing so. But I was happy with my new life. I loved Jesus and felt that even dying for Jesus would be a privilege.

Opposition to the Christian faith was only strongly enforced if someone was active in sharing their faith. It was evangelism the Communists had a real problem with. There were people from Orthodox and Catholic backgrounds who didn't suffer persecution. At the same time freedom fighters were sometimes sent to our group as spies to try to lure us to join their own anti-government cause.

In spite of all the harassment and intimidation, our little group continued to share the gospel at every opportunity. The wife of the town's governor came to faith, as did several teachers, hospital workers and many civil servants.

Bahlibi was another of our converts. Bahlibi was in his 30s and from the ministry of agriculture. He was smartly dressed and always smiling and joking. When we first met, he made fun of Jesus. But when he realised I was a Christian he apologised and expressed an interest in hearing more. He was preparing to get married, but his fiancé wrote him a letter dumping him. Bahlibi was heartbroken. I shared the gospel with him and he gave his life to Christ. He became so committed to the faith that he was frequently in and out of prison. A few years later he sadly died of stomach cancer.

I will always remember him. He had become such a generous, loving follower of Christ. He was always singing and often stayed with my parents in Asmara. He became almost part of the family. His death came as a shock. At first my family tried to hide it from me. I found myself asking, 'God, why did you allow Bahlibi to die?' Even today, I have no answer. He was such a strong follower of Jesus. He was just 34 years old. The world wasn't good enough for Bahlibi.

Sometimes there can be no answers to such questions, not in this life, anyway. We are called to live with the mystery and to put our trust in the goodness of God.

6

'BROTHER, I HAVE COME TO ARREST YOU'

Citizens were obliged to attend a Marxist indoctrination programme – brainwashing, essentially. Three times a week, Mondays, Wednesdays and Fridays, you had to attend these two-hour sessions in the town hall, running from five until seven in the morning. It was now 1980 and I was 24.

They would haul 200 of us in a room to yell curses at capitalism and shout our praises to Marxist-Leninism. 'Down with capitalism! Down with imperialism! Forward with Marxist-Leninism! Forward with our revolutionary government!'

Then the cadres would call on individuals to lead the crowd in chanting Communist slogans. 'Berhane,' the leader called to me. 'Lead us in the slogans.'

'No,' I replied. 'I will not.'

The cadre's expression darkened. 'Are you angry that I have exposed your Christian faith?' he demanded.

'No,' I said simply. 'If you will allow me, I will speak about it.'

'This is not a church!' he yelled. And after the meeting he demanded to know why I refused to lead the slogans. In turn, I asked him why he'd picked on me. But he'd already given me my answer. In Eritrea, many Christians were in prison because of their faith.

All that shouting worked up quite an appetite. After these sessions we would rush to grab some breakfast before heading off to work for the day.

One morning, I failed to turn up for the customary Communist shout-in. As a nursing assistant in the hospital, I had to go in early to relieve the night shift. And a local police officer was despatched to the hospital to arrest me. I knew him well. Gutama was a new convert to Christianity, who came to my house for discipleship studies. He was slim, in his 30s and usually happy. 'Brother, I have come to arrest you,' he said. I thought my policeman friend was joking, but his face told me otherwise.

Gutama had received a telegram from the town police department to pick me up and send me to Asmara by a military convoy. They would be waiting for me at 10 am.

My friend said he would leave me to get ready. And looking back I think he was giving me a chance to flee. But I didn't want to make a run for it; I was sure of my innocence. I asked the Lord, 'God, what are you going to do in this situation?' And I felt at peace. I told some of the nurses what was happening and they prepared food for me and got my medicine.

An hour later, Gutama returned with several other officers who took me away to begin the long journey to Asmara. Two schoolteachers were also in the truck, both men in their mid-20s. Like me, they'd been arrested. And like me, they'd not been told why.

Despite the sudden turn of events, my heart was full of peace. I was sure God had a purpose for me in all of this. I had my New Testament and sat in the back of the lorry reading Bible verses to these teachers. To begin with, they mocked me. But they were angry and scared. One kept repeatedly trying to light a cigarette, but each time, his match would blow out in the wind. He became increasingly agitated. He kept saying, 'I'm going to die. I will be tortured.' That thought did not enter my heart. I was at peace.

Just another day in Eritrea.

We travelled for about 50 miles and then had to stop in Dekemhare. There was fighting ahead and the rebels had blocked the road. We were stuck there for eight days. The police officers escorting us used the local horse stables as a makeshift prison cell and locked us inside. Fortunately, some Christians in the town knew me and were aware of my arrival. They visited us with food.

I spent those days singing and sharing the gospel with other prisoners. One song translates:

> *'You have not abandoned us, Lord,*
> *you have not forsaken us*
> *to the mercy of the enemy.'*

The prisoners joined in but replaced the word 'Lord' with EPLF.

As I sang, I felt the presence and assurance of God. I was even able to befriend the guards, who were from the Orthodox faith. 'God loves you,' I said, 'Jesus died for your sins. If you follow Him, he will take care of you. He will give you joy and peace.' I never had to force this upon them: mostly they came up to me to find out why I was always praising and singing.

There was a shortage of food while we were in Dekemhare, so I asked an officer if we could get something to eat. Perhaps he didn't realise I was a prisoner. In any event, we walked together two miles to the town centre, where we had lunch in a small restaurant. On the way back we hitched a lift on a horse and cart, a common enough form of transport, given the constant shortage of fuel. Then the officer asked me why I was travelling to Asmara. When I told him I was on my way to prison, he was surprised.

Once again, I'd been given the chance to flee, but had chosen to remain. Had I fled, the officer would have got in trouble, and I didn't want to spoil my testimony; I wanted to share with him about my faith in Christ. I knew God could intervene, but even if he chose not to rescue me, I prepared myself to be faithful even unto death.

Finding enough to eat was an everyday challenge. One day we had nothing and asked one of the guards to get us some food. The army commander told our escorts to shoot us! Fortunately, he only said it to keep us quiet. But later that day a Christian soldier, who knew me from Adi Keyh, came to see me and brought enough to feed all ten of us in that makeshift cell.

After eight days, the road had been cleared and we continued our journey. When we finally got to Asmara, I asked the police to contact my mother. She rushed to the police station just in time to see me before I was locked up. She waved from afar. I can see her now, crying, in her long dress with purple flowers and white headscarf. She clearly had no idea what was happening. This was the most distressing part, but I knew that God was in charge and felt sure He would intervene. It was not time for me to die.

I was able to find out a little more about why I was there. A policeman informed me that a man called Joseph had given them my name. I knew this Joseph. He was a teacher, and an atheist, and they'd arrested him in Adi Keyh where I had lived.

Back then, I had visited Joseph in jail. He was depressed and unresponsive. He said: 'These people are Communist. They know everything. You must confess everything you have in your heart.' Under torture, he had poured out the names of many people he knew – including, it seems, me.

From the police station I was transferred to the maximum-security centre called Wenjel Mirmera, where many Christian pastors have been locked up for years. It was built by the Italians during the Second World War. When I entered, I was taken into a hall, where there were 60-70 prisoners. Most wore bandages on their feet. They told me they had all been tortured. I asked them why. They laughed. 'The same thing will happen to you.'

'No,' I said. 'God will protect me.' Which made them laugh even louder.

7

THE GENTLE ASSASSIN

Torture was standard practice in Wenjel Mirmera. Often prisoners would confess to crimes they hadn't even committed. One health worker admitted under torture to giving medicine to opposition freedom fighters – and was executed.

Even so, I still felt relaxed and was able to sleep peacefully that first night in Wenjel Mirmera, though there was no bed, just a blanket on the floor. The next morning, they moved me to another cell with about 45 people.

It was overcrowded, with very little leg room, and infested with lice. The heat was stifling. Nearly all the prisoners were smoking, which made it even more suffocating, particularly as the only windows were high up in the ceiling. Some were gambling and dancing; some were just screaming. The noise was oppressive. I pulled the blanket over my head and began praying silently. A verse of Scripture came to mind: 2 Peter 2:7, where the Lord '…rescued righteous Lot (who was) greatly distressed by the sensual conduct of the wicked.'

In that cell were old, young and very young. There were serial killers, robbers, political activists and criminals of every kind. The new prisoners were expected to entertain the others. They asked me to sing a song. As I knew no secular songs, I sang a gospel song.

'Though I have no gold or silver,

my peace is great.

I may look weak and miserable,

but I am strong inside,

because I have Jesus.'

And after I finished, I explained what the song meant to me, as a vulnerable person with diabetes.

Prison is filled with sadness and fear. There was no due legal process: no trial, no legal representation – no justice. Some prisoners were never told what crimes they were supposed to have committed. They could release you without charge or leave you behind bars to rot. All without ever appearing in court. Who knew what would happen? Only God.

It was these prisoners who were vulnerable. They needed to know the love of God. These prisoners were here for interrogation and torture. And for some that would lead inevitably to execution. I never spoke about judgment. I spoke only about love. I shared from the scriptures and told my Christian story. And during that time, everyone was listening and coming for prayer.

In the night you talk to pass the time. The prisoner beside me was a member of the Eritrean People's Liberation Front, the EPLF. He told me he was an assassin. His name, as I recall, was Mehari.

This gentle man who was in his early 20s and who slept next to me, shoulder to shoulder, calmly informed me he'd killed 11 members of the Ethiopian security forces. He described himself as a *fedayeen*, one of the militia whose name in Arabic means those who are willing to sacrifice themselves. But he didn't act like a murderer.

One day the guards called for both of us and made us stand facing the wall in the compound. Then they ordered us to turn and face them. For a moment, I wondered if we were going to be executed. But instead of a rifle, we were confronted with a man with a camera who calmly took our pictures. The assassin looked a little like me, and I think they wanted to photograph us together to show to a witness for identification.

Mehari heard me speaking about Jesus and asked me whether God would forgive him if he said he was truly sorry. I assured him God would. We prayed together and he was touched. We spent the whole of that day talking about Jesus. I believe he became a Christian. Soon after he was executed. Others were also taken to be killed.

From then on, every evening I would read from the Psalms and sing gospel songs. As we sat together many of the prisoners asked me questions about God. This was a new experience for most of them and I was happy to be in the cell with them. This, I believed, was the reason God had brought me there.

One morning when we went outside for our ten-minute daily break, we found women prisoners. One was sitting on her own. She was a housemaid who'd been accused of stealing. She couldn't have been older than 18. She was wearing a blue floral skirt and had tears in her eyes. To try to force a confession, they'd tortured her feet and broken her bones. She was fearful and clearly in pain. Her foot was infected and stinking out her cell. It seemed there was no one who could clean the wound, so I offered to do so.

As I began to wash her foot, I saw fragments of bone poking out of her ankle. I said to the prison officer, 'This woman needs to go to hospital; otherwise she could lose her foot – or die of septicaemia.' Her torturer sent for a car. He said he would not trouble with an armed escort –because he knew the woman was innocent.

I was allowed to go with them in a blue VW minibus, and after we'd taken the girl to hospital we set off back to prison. The road took us through the town centre where the civilian driver stopped to go shopping. He left me in the car, apparently unaware that I was a prisoner. Again, it was a chance to flee, but again, something came into my heart about fulfilling God's purposes, so I stayed.

After about 20 minutes the driver returned and apologised for taking so long with his shopping. He took us back to the prison, where it seemed some of the officers hadn't realised I'd been to the hospital. They assumed I'd escaped and were searching for me, to interrogate me. And that was when they sent for me and when the torture began. Not the whip nor the electric shock machine. Just the log beneath my knees and the stick to my feet.

Everything in that torture room was geared up to torment you and instil you with fear, even before your torture began. But somehow, I was filled with a heavenly joy. I was able to continue singing and praying, which angered my interrogators all the more. And when I had that vision of Jesus, suffering and dying for me on the cross, taking my pain, His pain eclipsing my own, I fell silent.

My captors thought I'd fallen unconscious. My silence frustrated them almost as much as my singing. One said: 'I will kill him – I will shoot him with my gun.' But even then, I didn't stir. So they untied me and dragged me to another room, limping and barely able to walk. 'Can I have five minutes to pray?' I asked, and without waiting for their response, bowed down to do so. This made the sergeant so furious that he threw me back in the cell.

And I returned to that cell the only man in that room who still had hope. The Lord had allowed me to pass through suffering so that I could share in the sufferings of my fellow prisoners. And having gone through this ordeal, my own faith was transformed in that prison.

Some of my cellmates had been paralysed from the torture they'd been made to endure. Some had lost their toes from the beating. Everyone was bandaged, but me. Although my feet felt as though they had been burned with hot coals, I was not even bleeding, which is a mercy. As a diabetic, if I'd suffered an open wound in that dirty room, I would probably have lost my foot.

My ankle was fractured, and I was unable to walk for weeks. But even so, I rejoiced that God had protected me. The prisoners put oil on my feet and I worshipped Jesus. Many listened to me speak that evening, and as I praised Jesus, there were murmurs of, 'Amen! Amen!'

These prisoners were the reason I was there. Their days were numbered. When they selected the prisoners to die they carted them off in a lorry escorted by machine-gun Jeeps through a small village, and then on to a mass grave. It was clear to me what Jesus wanted. He didn't want me to live for myself, but to serve these others.

Later, I had to return to the hospital for insulin. A prison officer took me in a car. One of the nurses called my sister. We were able to talk for ages, as I waited for the prison car to return. When it didn't show up, my sister suggested the prison officer went to a payphone to call for another. It was yet another opportunity to escape. But again, although I had a chance to run, I remained. If I had escaped that prison officer would have been executed by firing squad.

Now having endured the torture and encountered Jesus, I became fearless and bold. My time behind bars taught me to love my enemies, and to persevere when things didn't go the way I wanted. It is true to say I experienced the presence of God every day.

Eventually each person in the prison knew about me. Some still tried to intimidate me, but I told them, 'I am ready to give my life; so don't try to scare me. I will not be scared.'

After about 16 days we were led out to army lorries waiting outside the prison, along with heavily armed soldiers. Some prisoners feared we were about to be executed. I was expecting to be released. Instead we were sent to Sembel prison, Wing 10 – reserved for prisoners on death row.

Sembel Prison was bigger and more modern. It was constructed from square black stone and ringed with guardposts. Cut into its large entrance was a smaller gate for people. And then an inner gate. Wire fences separated the wings, which housed 1,300 prisoners. I had never heard of anyone escaping this depressing place.

When we arrived, some of us had a chance to see our prison files. The heading on mine read: 'Top anti-revolutionary'! The charge was essentially treason, a crime punishable by death. I couldn't understand why this was on my file, or why I'd been thrown in with this group of people. Quietly in prayer I asked God to show me His purpose.

They shaved our hair and assigned us to cells. I was locked in a cell next to the health centre, because of my diabetes. This was a blessing. My cell had its own small courtyard. In the middle was a tiny patch of small yellow flowers that made me feel alive. Each day we would walk round and round this lively little patch for exercise. While encircling us in turn was a wire fence with a wall, overlooked by a security guard in a watchtower.

Wing 10 was secluded and out of sight of the other prisoners. We could be put to death without another soul knowing. Given that death was so close and some of those with me were about to be executed, I had serious work to do. So I was determined to carry on teaching the prisoners about God, just as I had done at Wenjel Mirmera.

Alongside me in the cell were members of the EPLF, the Marxist-Leninist rebel group, who were fighting to break Eritrea free from Ethiopia. These fighters were atheists, and even though they were prisoners of war, they acted as though they ran the place. The EPLF prisoners were always trying to put me down. I said to them: 'If you try to persecute me in prison, what will you do if you get into power?' The prison guards were just as aggressive and were constantly trying to scare us. But my faith was strong. I would not be bullied.

It had not always been this way.

As a boy, I was sick with diabetes and weak, and bullied constantly. But after I became a Christian, I was filled with a unique strength. Although outwardly I still looked weak, inwardly I was strong because I had Jesus in my heart. And wherever I was, I found that I would take charge.

Here at Sembel there was an Orthodox priest, himself a prisoner. He was bald with a long beard and in his 40s, but looked older. He spoke like an old man. Everybody just called him Priest. He led a daily litany, a chant about Mary, Michael and other saints. It was something I was not familiar with – but I knew if I was going to share the gospel of Christ I had to join in with these prayer times.

I read from the Psalms and did some preaching, followed by prayer. I prayed for the prisoners' release, and for God's protection from suffering or death. Sometimes I managed to talk one-to-one with another prisoner about Jesus Christ.

The prisoners could see how I was able to sleep untroubled and at ease. They told me my Bible readings brought them comfort, and my older sister Ghenet smuggled in Bibles and magazines to distribute among the prisoners. Ghenet was a tomboy. She was bold and fearless and like a second mother to me. My mother also came when she could.

In that cell was the man responsible for my arrest. Everyone hated Joseph because he'd named many innocent people during interrogation, resulting in their capture. The other prisoners were always cursing and insulting him. Joseph was in his late 20s, long-faced and bearded, quietly depressed and indifferent to the faith. I considered it my duty to help him and become his friend, but Joseph was determined to die.

He tried to stop himself breathing by putting his hand over his nose and mouth. He refused to eat or drink. I tried to feed him, chasing him like a toddler to see that he would not harm himself. But he'd reached the point where he had to be restrained. So I asked the health workers to give him intravenous fluid. Joseph was an atheist, but was clearly touched by the love I had shown him. We became close friends and studied the Bible together.

Joseph was taken to the psychiatric hospital for two months. Later, he asked to be returned to the wing where I was being held. But by then his mind was gone. He'd become like a child. He was sentenced to five years, probably for a crime he had never committed.

If they can break you, you will confess to anything. You would say anything to escape the torture – if you let them break you.

Prison is a place where every emotion and every human sin runs rampant. You experience hatred, anger, depression and cruelty. But it is also a place where you have the opportunity to learn how to love your enemies.

I learned to love Joseph. I learned to love even those who had tortured me. I learned to be patient, kind and generous. I found prison to be a place where you can exercise the fruit of the Spirit in Galatians 5: love, joy, peace, patience, kindness, goodness, faithfulness, gentleness and self-control.

Against such things no law nor punishment can prevail – not even a sentence of death in a dungeon in Eritrea.

8

THE FURIOUS COMMANDO

There were things that Sembel prison possessed, and things that Sembel prison did not possess, thank God. Sembel didn't have torture, but it did have executions. Most of all it had waiting, waiting, waiting.

Sembel was a place where prisoners waited to be transferred, either because they'd been sentenced or because they were awaiting sentence. Most were still waiting to find out, as prisoners were never officially charged. There were neither court appearances nor lawyers. Instead, a special army committee was convened to chew over their 'crimes' and dream up appropriate punishments. These included execution for asking for more food on the frontline.

Some of the prisoners were Eritrean freedom fighters who'd been captured as prisoners of war. Others were Communist leaders imprisoned for rocking the boat, or corruption. There were Ethiopian soldiers who'd committed crimes while on active service. And, finally, somewhere in that mix were genuine criminals. But most of those incarcerated in Sembel had been thrown there for taking a political or religious stance that rubbed the government up the wrong way.

So they waited and waited. And periodically an officer would read out a list of names, and those called would follow those officers out, whether to be released or executed, they had no idea.

So when their names were called, they didn't know whether to celebrate or cry.

Only later would we find out what happened to those whose names had been read out. Those who were released would send letters or food parcels to their prison friends. Those who were executed were never heard from again.

The prisoners' food parcels were welcome. Prison food was injera bread made from poor quality sorghum. It was inedible, so we kept it in the sun to sell to local beer makers. We lived off the family food parcels which were delivered three days a week. Everything we got, we shared. Half the prisoners never received a thing from their families, so whatever we received was shared by all. And we had more than enough to eat, thanks to our families.

I was often the target of jibes from freedom fighters, who were usually strongly anti-religious. But I never feared them. Their hostility was the devil's way to try to distract me from sharing the good news of Jesus. But I also came into conflict with the Communists who had fallen out of favour. They tried to stop me preaching by reporting me to those in charge.

One night, two political prisoners, Michael and Yemane, came to where I was sleeping and took my Bible. When I opened my eyes, I saw them reading it. To my surprise, they apologised for reading my Bible without my permission. They then prayed the Lord's Prayer together and went to sleep. Michael was a CEO for a drug import company. He'd been giving money to the rebel EPLF. Yemanei who worked in the post office, had also been funding the guerrillas. Both were in their 30s.

The next morning Michael was sentenced to two years and Yemane was put to death. Dozens of people were executed that day, four from my own cell. The whole place fell into a deep silence. No-one spoke, and many refused to eat.

That evening, after the doors were locked, we all gathered to pray. I'd been sharing from the Psalms and read Psalm 23, 'The Lord is my Shepherd'. Soon, I reached the verse 'Even though

I walk through the valley of the shadow of death, I will fear no evil, for you are with me,' (Psalm 23:4).

'When he wrote that, David was in a situation like ours,' I told the prisoners. 'He was in the shadow of death, but he said, "I will fear no evil, for you are with me." God is with us.'

One of the prisoners asked me to sing, which I was always happy to do – I love singing. I sang about Christ's love for us. And just after I'd finished, the door opened. It was the prison manager. Fear filled the room that he was about to reel off a second batch of names for execution. Some of the prisoners started crying out to God. But the prison manager made a short speech about how the Communist government was kind and merciful. Twenty-nine prisoners had been given a two-year sentence; six had been given five years; and finally four would remain for an indefinite period.

My name was not on the list and people wondered what would happen to me. It looked as though I was going to be in Sembel for some time! But I was okay with that: I still knew God was keeping me there for a purpose.

Many of the prisoners had been traumatised in various ways and fighting often broke out between them. One ex-soldier had been accused of treason and was awaiting execution. He'd been an Ethiopian commando, trained by the Israelis, who had deserted to join the EPLF. He was waiting too – for the President's signature on his death warrant.

This ex-commando was tall, powerfully built and constantly showed his anger by cursing those around him. His feet were permanently chained to restrain him, and I felt pity for him. I tried to share the gospel with him, but he was strongly opposed to the faith. Somehow, he managed to appeal against his sentence, which was changed to life imprisonment. Despite those chains, he got into plenty of fights.

By now, some of the prisoners looked on me as a kind of priest and asked me to mediate between this furious ex-soldier and the others. They called me Priest, Father, Pastor – even though I was just a 24-year-old boy.

There was another prisoner who heeded the gospel message of reconciliation. He knelt before this ex-commando and begged his forgiveness. But the commando's bitterness ran too deep. So the other prisoner did something extraordinary to prove his genuine desire for reconciliation. He told this trained killer: 'I can see you are desperate to fight me. I will pray you get released so you can.'

From time-to-time security officers came in to search for Bibles. The only prisoners allowed to read the scriptures were those under sentence of death. I tried to hide my Bible by giving it to the ex-commando. But he betrayed me and handed my Bible to the officers. I begged them to give it back: 'You can do whatever you like, but I will not let you have it.'

The prison officer said, 'Trust me, I will give your Bible back.' But he was lying. Fortunately, I didn't have to wait too long for another, as my sister Ghenet was still boldly smuggling Bibles into the prison in food baskets.

A group of Ethiopian soldiers in the cell had been imprisoned for asking for more food on the front line. That was their crime. And for that they were on death row.

One of them, Taddesse, a health care worker, was a Christian. When he saw me praying and preaching, he confessed his faith and we immediately bonded as friends. Soon after, Taddesse was summoned to be executed. He left me with this Bible verse: 'If in Christ we have hope in this life only, we are of all people most to be pitied.' (1 Corinthians 15:19).

One day a group of Eritrean prisoners of war were brought into the cell, straight from the battlefield. They were tired and dirty and their heads were down. No one wanted to talk to them. The Ethiopians, of course, hated them at once and wanted nothing to do with them, while the other Eritreans feared repercussions because of them.

I volunteered to take food to them and to sit and talk with them. I asked them what had happened, and they were happy to see someone who was unafraid to show them hospitality. I was simply following Christ's command to love others.

I continued to preach as much as I could. Estephanos was about to be transferred out of the prison. He'd been jailed for supporting the Eritrean Peoples' Liberation Front. Just before he left, he came over and told me he believed the Bible was God's word and that it had been a real comfort to him.

Some didn't believe a word but just listened quietly. Solomon was one of those. Twenty years later, I visited a church I helped to plant. The pastor wanted to introduce me to one of his members who said he knew me. It was the former ELF fighter, Solomon, who'd been in that cell. He told me: 'I listened to your preaching – and I gave my life to Jesus Christ.'

9

NEWS OF MY EXECUTION

In Sembel, I came upon another prisoner called Berhane Asmelash. He looked a little like me, too, though this Berhane was a few years older. I'd met him once before, years earlier at my cousin's house. He'd been working in Tigray with World Vision. My namesake was in prison for giving financial support to Tigray rebels. He worked in the library at Sembel, and I made an excuse to go there and catch up with him. When I first met him, he hadn't been a Christian, but he'd subsequently come to faith in Christ. I was thrilled.

The next day the prison registrar began to reel off yet another list of names of prisoners to be executed. Mine was among them. But another prisoner told the registrar to check the middle name, as it might not be the correct Berhane Asmelash. The registrar told me to stay where I was until they resolved this confusion. It was the other Berhane Asmelash who was taken: I never saw him, or any of the others in that group again.

When news got out about the executions my mother thought I had been killed. She came to the city hospital, where prisoners were being treated, to find out. She knew there was another Berhane Asmelash in Sembel, so it was a 50/50 chance. I guessed she would come to the prison, and I asked the nurse to send me to the hospital for a check-up, in case my mother was there. And when I jumped off the lorry, sure enough, there was my mother waiting at the gates. She was so happy when she saw me: 'You're alive? You don't deserve this. You are a good boy.' This was what she always said.

My sister Ghenet had smuggled in a magazine from the Billy Graham organisation. It reached Daniel, a prisoner I'd never met. Daniel passed me a note saying he'd appreciated an article on the Apostle John in exile on the island of Patmos. The writer had spoken about living in isolation and yet knowing God. Daniel and I regularly exchanged letters and finally met at the clinic. Eventually he was released and became a committed Christian. He remained one of my best friends for many years.

I got into the habit of starting my days at five in the morning. I would read my Bible until seven, then take a short break. I used to spend most of my waking hours singing. Some of the prisoners thought me strange, but many would ask deep spiritual questions.

I also tried to encourage the church outside the prison and started writing letters to my house church. Once I quoted from the Book of Revelation: 'Do not fear what you are about to suffer. Behold, the devil is about to throw some of you into prison, that you may be tested, and for ten days you will have tribulation. Be faithful unto death, and I will give you the crown of life.' (Revelation 2:10). Many of my letters were censored by the authorities.

One of my biggest challenges behind bars was my health. I needed insulin and had to test my blood to keep my blood sugar under control. I also needed to eat regularly. But one of the officers refused me insulin. I said there was no way I could continue without it. He replied: 'I don't care. You're a criminal. You're here to be punished, not to be treated.'

Fortunately, one of the nurses allowed me to go to the hospital. Hospital was less crowded, I could sleep more easily, the food was better, and the nurses were friendly too. It was also the best way to communicate with my family, as my mother and sisters could visit, and when my father was able to take time off work, he came too.

During my 11th month of incarceration, I woke up in hospital at 5am as usual for my morning devotions. While I was praying, I saw in my imagination the iron bars melting at the window.

Was it a dream? Could it be true? It left me with a strange mix of hope and happiness. During breakfast I told some of the other prisoners that I had a feeling I was about to be released. They just scoffed.

But at lunchtime a soldier called my name, and the message came that I was to be set free. I just had to get my father to bail me out. The following morning I was free to go home! I'd been arrested in April and now it was March.

My family were overjoyed. All my aunties, friends and neighbours crowded into our house for the celebration. It was as though someone had been raised from the dead. How we feasted! Every day, people would bring food and drink. Everyone in the neighbourhood came. Nobody believed I had been guilty. Everyone knew that prison was not for criminals.

But freedom was not without its difficulties. Prison had become my routine and I treated it like a job. I'd set my mind on the possibility that I might never be released. I'd accepted prison and settled there. And after 11 months, I was well on the way to becoming institutionalised. I was happier inside prison than out.

What did excite me was being able to go to church again. But very soon I became aware of the many divisions within the congregation. I was shocked because it just wasn't like that in prison. When people are free, they feel they have the luxury of picking meaningless conflicts.

I befriended a group of Ethiopians who invited me to their fellowship. My father was surprised that I was so forgiving and trusting of Ethiopians after everything that had happened to me. But hatred was out of the question. Even when Jesus was on the cross, He forgave his enemies. And He commanded us to forgive, too. That's why I was able to love Joseph, who'd betrayed me and to take care of him. And that's why I was able to smile and talk to the prison guard who took my Bible. Nasty or not, I was able to befriend them.

Somebody once said, 'If you want to learn to hate, go to prison.' But for me, prison was the place where I learned to love my enemies.

Love is not a feeling, it's a choice. If my enemies hit me or persecute me, I will not leave it up to them to decide whether I will love them or not. The decision to love or to hate another human being is under my control.

If I were to meet my torturer today, I would try to understand him. I would ask him how he felt while he was torturing my feet. I would ask him where his anger came from. 'You don't know me,' I would say, 'so why were you so angry with me?' But I would not judge him. I have no idea what this man has gone through. But I have already made the choice to forgive him.

There was a system in prison for torture and someone had to do it. I will never hold a grudge, not even against Eritrea's present government. I hate what they do, but I do not hate them personally. I have trained myself to forgive. I ask myself, what would Jesus do? And I try to follow in His footsteps. Jesus was ridiculed, persecuted and executed, but still He forgave. And if we are to be forgiven, we must forgive too.

10

OPPOSITION AND OPPORTUNITY

After I was released from prison, I found it difficult to cope with ordinary life. The memories kept flooding back: the torture, the execution of close friends, the prisoners I'd left behind, the suffering of their families. In the first few days, every time a car stopped outside, I expected that to be followed by a knock at the door.

My dreams were filled with nightmares, and my nightmares were filled with the faces of all the prisoners who'd been executed. I would find myself among those dead in my dreams, or back in the torture room, or with those who'd been left paralysed and in pain. And that trauma remained. I struggled for several years, but the Ethiopians I met in church were supportive.

I realised I had to do something about my education and my future. I managed to get a post in the Accident and Emergency department in the hospital in Asmara, working shifts 24-hours on and 48 hours off. I knew that finishing secondary education would not be easy, having been out of it for five years, but to get to university I would need to put in two more years of schooling. So, I studied while I worked. Thankfully, I did well in school and was one of the few who passed their university entrance exam.

Now it was down to the government to assign me to a medical school. There were only two in the country, one in

Addis, the other in Gonder in the north-west. Wherever I was sent, I wanted to be sure it was God's will. In September 1982 I was accepted into medical school in Gonder, the ancient religious city and former capital of Ethiopia.

Gonder is surrounded by mountains and trees, and amply supplied by streams. This green city is known for its immense 17th Century Portuguese-style castle and its many historic Orthodox churches. My father had been based in Gonder from 1935 to 1941, when he was serving in the Italian army, before being captured by the British.

However, some who knew the area well tried to warn me off. And some prophets in the church told me not to go. But was that the Lord, or just the fears of men? One nurse, whom I trusted, reminded me that God never makes mistakes. She urged me to carry on and go. It was the reassurance that I needed.

At the time, the Ethiopian government was heavily influenced by the Soviet Union and Cuba. Ethiopia clung to Marxist-Leninist doctrines. It was suspicious of supposedly Western religions, including Pentecostals and Evangelicals. As for the Lutheran denomination, it was too large and too-well established for the government to oppose it wholesale.

The Orthodox Church was generally tolerated because it was woven into the fabric of society – half the country would call themselves Christians, and most of those would say they were Orthodox. The authorities regarded Orthodox Christians as generally compliant background believers who had their uses.

The Communists stirred up their hardliners to persecute the Pentecostals and Evangelicals. Those who became agents of this government-driven cleansing process seem to have forgotten the example of Jesus. Jesus chose to invite, rather than force people to follow him.

The Communists demanded utter obedience and complete allegiance to the party. The party maintained there was no God.

The Evangelicals, of course, firmly disagreed and were determined to share their faith in the God they believed in, which put them in contention with the authorities. And because they did share their faith, their numbers were growing. The government shut down every Evangelical church by decree, and closely monitored the others.

And then it fired an unmistakable warning salvo across the bows of the Lutherans. The President of the Ethiopian Evangelical Church, a member church of the Lutheran World Federation, was assassinated.

The Rev Dr Giduna Tumsa was widely respected for his work in promoting peace and justice in Ethiopia. It's widely believed that the Mengistu military regime was implicated in his assassination.

The previous year, Dr Tumsa had given an interview to the BBC, in which he spoke about the political situation in Ethiopia and the human rights abuses committed by the regime. He also talked about the role of the church in advocating for justice and human rights in Ethiopia.

The interview was seen as a powerful statement of opposition to the regime and brought Rev Dr Tumsa to the attention of the international community. He was already a target before the interview and his growing popularity among the Ethiopian people could have been seen as a threat to the regime's hold on power.

Dr Tumsa was arrested then later released, after the Lutheran World Federation appealed to President Nyerere in Tanzania for help. But even then Dr Tumsa refused to leave his church and his country. He chose to remain in harm's way, declaring: 'Here is my church and my congregation. How can I, as a church leader, leave my flock at this moment of trial? I have again and again pleaded with my pastors to stay on.'

He quoted 2 Corinthians 5:15: '"Christ died for all that those who live should no longer live for themselves but for him who died for them and was raised again'" adding, 'Never ever will I escape.'

Dr Tumsa was captured by soldiers and strangled. He became known as the Dietrich Bonhoeffer of Africa. His assassination was a tragic loss for the Ethiopian church and for the people of Ethiopia. His legacy of courage, faith, and commitment to justice continues to inspire Ethiopians today.

If the leader of a church in the international spotlight could be murdered for his views, what protection was there for ordinary Ethiopians critical of government policy? Thousands of young people were rounded up and thrown into secret prisons, where many were executed and their bodies dumped in the streets.

Such scenes were said to be commonplace in Gonder, where I was heading.

Nevertheless, along with three other medical students we boarded a DC3 Dakota and set out. The plane itself seemed ominous. Rainwater leaked into the fuselage and its door had to be held shut with a piece of wire. Somehow this ramshackle aircraft got us to Gonder and we touched down about ten miles from the university. I wondered what would await us.

I was told the governor of Gonder was cruel and didn't like Christians. He'd arranged for the town to turn out to throw stones at the Full Gospel Church. He'd had the members beaten and gave them 24 hours to get out of town. By now, I didn't know if there would be any church left in Gonder or any Christians at the university. But I resolved not to hide my faith.

The old hospital had been established by Americans but was now run by a staff from East Germany, which supplied most of our teachers. The hospital boasted some 400 beds, medical, paediatric, maternity, gynaecology, surgical and orthopaedic wards, as well as a nursing school: Gonder Medical Science College Hospital.

My roommate's name was Michael. He was short and fair-skinned with big eyes. Soon after we arrived, I was sitting on my bed, when Michael pulled out a Bible from his bedside drawer and briefly prayed, before quickly hiding his Bible away again. I asked him: 'Are you a Christian?' He hesitated. I said, 'I ask you because I am a Christian.' And he hugged me.

He said there was a Lutheran Church in the town that met at 7 am. I asked him whether it was safe to practice our faith here. Michael gave me a look: 'Not really.' In fact, it was illegal for college students to go to church.

Nevertheless, the following Sunday Michael took me to the Lutheran Church, Mekane Jesus (Place for Jesus). It was stone built and large enough to hold 120. But there were only seven inside, and most of these were the minister's family. Even so, I was happy to be there.

The minister preached the gospel and the little congregation sang. The old organ was covered with dust and clearly neglected. I eyed it up and asked the minister if I could play on Sundays. He was delighted, and when I told him my family were Lutherans, he invited me to join the preaching rota, along with the minister himself and an elderly evangelist.

I got to preach every third Sunday in Amharic, the Ethiopian national language, and for the first few Sundays the people just laughed at my accent. But we formed a choir and numbers began to grow. And eventually, this empty church became full. Most Evangelicals came to our church, and they were joined by the Pentecostals. So, gradually these Lutherans changed their flavour to become more evangelical and more pentecostal.

The only union permitted at the college was the Communist Union. The Christian Union was forced to meet in secret. Its leader had been arrested and I was warned of the risk. Its members met for Bible study in the evenings. On my first visit we met in the Lutheran church in the dark. The others kept their identities secret, because I was new and could have been a spy. We had to do the Bible study from memory, and afterwards, left the building two-by-two.

Along with my roommate Michael and Henok, another student we started a Sunday prayer meeting at the home of a Christian family. We were few in number, but I remembered the saying, one plus Jesus is always a majority. I knew Jesus was on my side; the fear I'd experienced when I arrived in Gonder was gone, and my heart was filled with joy. We prayed for God to help us to be bold in sharing the gospel.

During my second semester we met a small group of Christian doctors who'd come to the university for internship. We started a fellowship in their room and studied Christian discipleship, which was desperately needed, as all of us were inexperienced in underground Christian ministry. One of these three interns was a gospel singer. Another, Tesfaye, was in his fourth year of study. He was more mature and was leading this fellowship.

After dark, Tesfaye took me to the Lutheran church to meet other members of the University Christian Union. There were three Bible study groups: one gathered with a Christian family in the town, another at the Lutheran church, where we met in the dark with the lights off; a third gathered in the forest during the day, mostly on Sundays. Another group met for fellowship and prayer in the Interns' room.

Tesfay took me to the forest to meet other Christians from the campus. They were all were new faces to me. We had regular prayer and Bible study under those trees – Full Gospel, Baptists, Mennonites and others, all worshipping together. Persecution always brings unity. In the underground church in Eritrea, there are few denominational divisions. When Christians meet in secret they generally come from different churches. And in prison, nobody asks which church you are from. It is only freedom that brings the luxury of division.

11

AN OVERWHELMING SENSE OF UNEASE

As we continued to meet beneath the trees, from time-to-time, farmers with sheep or passers-by stumbled upon us and stared suspiciously and we were worried they might report us to the authorities. But our numbers continued to grow, so much so that we found it difficult to continue to meet in the open-air.

That first year was hard: only one family was willing to let us use their home. A few years earlier, the authorities had raided the houses of Christians and beaten them badly. So, when the Christian Union started to grow and challenged local believers to open their homes for Bible study, everyone was scared. The locals spelled it out: Go away, we don't want any more trouble.

We continued to be open about our faith on the campus. In the dining hall we would say the blessing openly: 'Jesus, we thank you for this food and pray for those who are hungry.' Everyone in that hall knew we were praying. Some of the students warned me to be careful.

But our numbers continued to grow and rumours began to circulate around the town. One day the Lutheran minister warned me the governor of Gonder was after me and urged me not to share my faith. I told him I could not change.

In that first year at college we studied general subjects including philosophy, political economy, maths and English. I managed to pass with good grades, although the exams were tough and many students were dismissed. When I returned for my second year we began our medical studies proper: anatomy, physiology and biochemistry. I was a happy man.

But running underground Bible studies under cover of darkness in the church and in the open air beneath the trees was becoming a challenge.

That second year I met a nursing student, Yehzbealem, whose family lived in the town. She'd been attending an Orthodox youth group and wanted to know more about the Christian faith. She accepted Jesus as her personal saviour and invited me to her home to meet her mother and brothers. Eventually our fellowship started using her house for our quarterly get-togethers. Thirty people were coming, so it became even more important to take care to arrive and leave discreetly.

I'd speak to people in the street and ask them if they'd read the Bible and, if so, what they thought of its message. One or two were coming to faith every week. Most of the houses we used for Bible studies belonged to these newly converted secret believers – most of whom were becoming Christians through the testimony of students.

A woman with a street lifestyle turned up at church with her sister. Over coffee she admitted they'd been waiting for a man to pick them up and take them to a local night club. No man had taken the bait, so after hanging around all night they had come to church instead! They had come to the right place.

I asked the two sisters if they read their Bible. No. Never. I took them to an outside café and they opened their hearts to the Lord. Both sisters gave their lives to Jesus that morning. They invited me to their house and introduced me to their parents, who were delighted to see their daughters back home at a sensible, respectable time! Their father, who was elderly, died soon after, but their other sisters and their mother came to faith together.

Newer cell churches started to mushroom every month and the numbers of believers multiplied, both on the student campus and in the town. As more people started coming to Christ the authorities became more determined to arrest us.

A man who worked on the university campus as a carpenter invited me to his house, but when I turned up to see him, he was out. His heavily pregnant wife was carrying water from the river in a 20-litre container. I asked her if I could give her a hand. She was touched by my help and when I started to tell her the good news about Jesus she joyfully accepted – and then invited all her neighbours to come and hear!

There were seven families in the block where she lived and some became Christians. I learned from this that a little kindness can make a big difference in people's lives. That is why Jesus challenges us to *do* the word as well as to preach it.

Everyday life in Gonder was an adventure. I went with a friend to Gorgora, a town some 40 miles away, on the shore of Lake Tana. We visited some Christians and stayed for a few days. On the way home my friend told me the story of a Christian woman who'd lost her husband and, because she couldn't support her five children, opened a bar. Bars were often seedy places in Ethiopia so I suggested we paid her a visit to see if we could help her.

It was about 7am when we arrived. The woman had just got up and was rubbing her eyes. After our talk, she reaffirmed her faith and decided to close the bar and rent out her rooms to Christians. Years later I found a full-blown church meeting inside her courtyard.

Soon after we were leading a Bible study at her house and were invited to stay overnight. But I was unable to shake off an overwhelming sense of unease that I couldn't really explain. It was as though someone was following me. There was nothing I could see, but I could feel it.

So I decided to take a taxi and head back to Gonder. The next day one of the women at the Bible study came to see me at the university. She said that. at about 2am, security forces had knocked on the other woman's door. They were looking for 'the Pentecostal preacher'. They meant me. They took all her Bibles and stripped the walls of Bible verses. I was relieved that I'd followed my instincts. It must have been the Holy Spirit's guidance.

Another challenge was the threat from 'fake' Christians. People would ask to join us, and sometimes it was with the motive of finding out about our secret Bible study group. So, we couldn't trust anyone.

Every new believer had to be kept separate from the rest, so if they reported us, they would only be able to report on one person – the one who was looking after them. As we became more confident that their conversion was genuine, the new believer would be introduced to a group of five. Only later would he be allowed to join the larger fellowship.

There was one person I was particularly suspicious of – Mefsun. I wondered if he was a double agent. He continued to be in the youth leadership of the Communist party, even after he'd become an active member of our fellowship. Michael, my roommate, was the one who led him to Christ. Michael wanted to bring him into the fellowship, but I refused to let him join the larger group. Instead, I assigned him to Michael's small group.

When we were due to meet, I would only tell Mefsun the same day, so if he were a spy, he'd have no time to inform on us. But as I got to know Mefsun I grew to trust him. He proved to be genuine. He even told us when we were in danger of being raided and ought to change our venue. Mefsun is now in Stockholm, pastoring a church.

We were always being spied on by the Communists. One day the city's party members came to our college and called a meeting in the dining hall. Mefsun had warned us they were coming. Their main aim was to stir up opposition to Christians on the campus, to provoke the other students to react.

The Communist leader gave a speech, claiming they'd identified eight Christian leaders they planned to take action against, and they called on the students to help them. They said: 'There are followers of a new religion here, who are spies for the CIA.' But the students only laughed. They knew very well that the accusations being hurled against us were lies. Even the students who weren't so sure about our faith knew for certain we weren't spies.

Instead, the students began to heckle the Communists, shouting over them and causing disruption. They fired question after question, demanded better food and a colour television. And the Communist himself, who'd tried to turn all these students against us became a Christian two months later, when one of the nurses shared her faith with him.

Yet still the Communists kept trying. The wife of the provincial party chairman came to the outpatient department, under the pretence of being sick. Her husband had been a key instigator of persecution against the Christians. She asked me to visit her. And despite the risks, I agreed. It would be a great opportunity to reach out to her husband – the very person who had vowed to destroy us – and share with him the love of the Lord.

So I went to her house and explained the gospel. We prayed together and she gave her life to Jesus. Later that evening when I shared with my friends what had happened they were furious! 'Are you crazy? What will you do if her husband finds you at his house? He will kill you!' But despite their concern I was not afraid.

I was also conducting Bible studies at the house of the deputy town mayor. He was against the Christian faith but his wife was a devout Christian. Then the wife of another Communist leader invited me to her house and introduced me to her husband. She gave her life to Christ and her Communist husband became my friend. But he told me that were he to give his life to Jesus he would be in trouble with the government. He said, 'I am happy for my wife to be a Christian, but I am not ready at this moment.'

This was life with Jesus, and far from being afraid, my heart was filled with joy. I could identify with the Apostle Paul, who told the Corinthians, 'A wide door for effective work has opened for me, and there are many adversaries.' (1 Corinthians 16:9).

The persecution reached its highest pitch after Alemu, one of the most prominent and popular students at university was converted and started to openly confess his faith. Alemu was an ex-army officer who was an alcoholic and had been struggling to finish his medical studies. I don't think he would have finished if he hadn't come to faith in the Lord.

After Alemu's conversion the university resolved to suspend some of the Christian students. During my summer break the principal's secretary, who was a secret believer, phoned me in Asmara, to tell me the administration was poised to take action, if I continued my preaching.

When I returned for my final year, even before I completed my registration, I was sent to see the Principal. Principal Malede, who was in his 60s, told me I'd been observed preaching to people in the city and on the university campus. And this, he informed me, was illegal in a revolutionary country like Ethiopia. I'd managed to offend the Communists, the Orthodox and the Catholics. All complained that I was converting their members.

'You are here to study not to preach. Preaching is illegal,' he said. 'You are spoiling people.'

'Look at Alemu,' I replied, 'he was an alcoholic. He was always drunk.'

'It is worse for him to be a Christian,' said the Principal. 'Your religion has no boundaries, no ethnicity and no country. I want you to write a statement that you will never again share your faith or convert anyone.' He was furious.

To back him up, the Vice Pesident bustled into his office. He was a Muslim. He said I would have to leave.

The Principal issued an ultimatum: if I wanted to stay at the university I had to promise not to convert anyone in the town or on campus. He handed me a piece of paper and asked me to write a statement and sign it.

I muttered I would think about it and left his office wondering what to do. I didn't sleep at all that night. Two friends, Michael and Henok. joined me in prayer. During that night we shared from the scripture about Moses' story. In the end, I was convinced to stay firm and I decided to write a short note to the Principal, saying, 'I will not preach about *religion*, but I will never stop talking about my Saviour and Lord, Jesus Christ.'

The Principal was disgusted and tried to convince me to change what I had written. I refused.

The following morning, I was suspended from the university for a year. The pretext they used was that I had scored a D in one of my subjects. It wasn't true. My grades were Bs. Our Professor of Paediatrics had been ordered to give the Christians Ds. Another Christian was also marked down and suspended along with me. I could bring myself to accept the suspension, but it was harder to accept the deception behind it.

Yet, strange as it may sound, I was still filled with joy: I felt both relief and fulfilment. If it was God's will, somehow I would still become a medical doctor. My ambitions lay elsewhere: in church planting, evangelism, discipleship and speaking up on behalf of prisoners. That is where my real passion lay. I believed medical training would open closed doors in Eritrea and give me access. But it was merely a means to an end. And that end, as well as the means lay in God's hands.

The Apostle Paul wrote, 'Indeed, all who desire to live a godly life in Christ Jesus will be persecuted.' (2 Timothy 3:12). For me, living a double life was not an option. I had to choose to worship God or the enemy. Sometimes the enemy's strategies are subtle and can raise doubts in our hearts, but I was pretty sure I was following God's guidance. When I returned home some friends and family branded me a religious fanatic, but I knew what I was doing, and didn't regret it one bit. I knew God had a purpose for my life.

12

'YOU WILL NEVER SEE YOUR MOTHER AGAIN'

During my year of suspension, Emmanuel Church in my hometown Asmara took me on as an evangelist and assistant to the pastor. The church had been planted by the Sudan Interior Mission (SIM). This was the Sunday school I went to as a child. It held good memories. I'd studied music there, played volleyball and basketball. And all the youths from the neighbourhood had gathered there for activities and sport.

The SIM missionaries who planted the church had been forced to evacuate Eritrea in 1974 during the war. The church had now come under the umbrella of Kale Hiwot, whose name meant Word of life. Its western equivalent would have been an evangelical free church. There was no liturgy or set service and the only adornment was a large, simple, wooden cross.

We composed our own choruses and accompanied them in the Eritrean style on an instrument with five strings. To western ears our music is a little like jazz, often in the minor key. And the rhythm can change halfway through. When we sing, people raise their hands. Sometimes we dance, clapping and jumping. But although the music is a far cry from that heard in churches in Europe, the sentiment of the worship is the same. One of our home-grown choruses went:

'I love you from my heart.

I choose you alone.

What else is there for me, but you, my Jesus?

You are everything for me.'

The small congregation of 24 were people who'd been caught up in the fighting and whose lives were a struggle. The church was stagnating and failing to attract new members. So I took charge of a youth group who were already coming to church on midweek evening services. It drew in many young people, including some from the Orthodox Church. And over that year, we added 32 new members.

By now I was 30, and that September I was due to go back to university for my final year. But first I travelled to Addis Ababa, to attend an underground house-church conference. I stayed at the home of a woman evangelist named Tsehay. Tsehay was in her 30s and always smiling, with a dimple in her cheek. She was a godly woman who became a mentor to me. When she shared the gospel she inspired me.

One morning, while I was praying in my bedroom, I had a strong feeling about my mother, who I really missed. I had a picture of her, just sitting in her chair. The sense of her presence filled my heart, like a heavy burden. After breakfast I told Tsehay. She had felt it too. She said she'd been scared to tell me but had a strong sense that my mother would soon go to be with the Lord. Tsehay insisted that I should leave the conference. 'Stop your ministry. Stay with your mother and give her your time. You will never see her again,' she told me.

So I duly bought a plane ticket and returned to Asmara. My mother was happy to see me, but she seemed fine. I started wondering, 'Why am I here?' My mother certainly didn't look as though she was about to die. But one morning, about a week later, my mother didn't get out of bed. 'I feel sick,' she said.

The government hospital would not admit her and the private hospital had no doctors. We took her there anyway. What else could we do? She had a burst bile duct and had developed peritonitis. She quickly became critical. Every day she went further downhill.

I was at her bedside along with her best friend and my sister Abeba. My mother was gasping and they sent me home because they didn't want me to see her die. I said goodbye and kissed her. She was 70. My father was at home with my youngest sister Bisrat. He wanted us to pray for my mother's healing, but I knew her time had come. I prayed: 'If she dies, Lord, accept her in your arms.'

Bisrat cried: 'No!' But as soon as we'd finished praying a car pulled up. Bisrat rushed out. It was the ambulance, which had brought us her body to bury. She had died within two weeks of developing that illness.

For me it seemed the end of the world. Everything turned dark. I was asking God why he had allowed it. And I blamed myself, thinking I could have taken her to a better doctor – but there were no 'better' doctors in Eritrea.

We arranged her funeral within a couple of days. Many friends came, including the pastor and the choir. We built a tent and they came for three days from different churches to sing and to preach. So many sermons! And not all of them were helpful. They rebuked us for being sad. 'You are making God angry,' they said. 'God is just.' Our friends were saying Christians shouldn't complain, but only sing, praise God and rejoice.

Every sermon upset me. People meant well. They were showing their concern, but they'd failed to understand that getting angry with God is not a problem. Anger doesn't mean a lack of faith. If we're in a relationship with God our Father we have the right to tell Him how we feel.

By then my suspension was over and I was due to start my final year in medical College. I was more than ready to leave this place of sadness. However, I took that sadness with me. The crushing loneliness and grief did not leave me for a year. And when I next headed back to Asmara, as the taxi drew near our home, I couldn't control my tears.

I now understand that in the grieving cycle, shock is followed by denial, and that acceptance begins at the funeral. This acceptance is followed by a celebration of the person's life. And that's when you begin to feel better.

But I was stuck in the final phase of denial. I was unable to fully accept my mother's death. Had I been there at my mother's last breath, it might have been different. But at the funeral, I felt as though I was only burying a casket.

With hindsight, I realise I should have insisted on staying with my mother until she died. And I should have delayed returning to the medical school. I could have talked everything through with my family and friends.

And to those Christians who came and tried to comfort us, I would say, put yourself into the grieving person's shoes and be sure you understand the true meaning of the scriptures you speak. Today, when I take funerals, I carefully weigh every word. I take care when I speak to a family in mourning. We must never judge them. We must be sensitive to their situation. But what happened over my mother's death left me angry with everyone.

13

FROM KINDNESS TO CRUELTY

So I returned to university to register for my final year. But I was heartbroken and had lost my confidence. In spite of the grief, I continued to preach in the church and to lead the fellowship. But as the months went by, I still missed my mother. And at the same time, I had to prepare for my final exam.

I carried on ministering in the town and the Christian fellowship on campus, although in the second semester I began to hand over most of my responsibilities to younger Christians.

A new governor had been assigned to the province. Ali Musa was even crueller than his predecessor. He had a reputation for killing hundreds of civilians and for arresting Ethiopian Christians. Ali Musa had been teaching the farmers. One farmer had said, 'I don't understand.' So Ali Musa explained again. Again, the farmer said, 'I still don't understand.' So Ali Musa said, 'You don't understand because you're an anti-revolutionary.' And he shot him.

In the south of the country he arrested members of the Full Gospel Church, including a young pastor. The pastor later described how Ali Musa had made the women remove their tops and beat their breasts with a whip. The pastor called him a monster, and Ali Musa knocked him out cold with his gun.

Astonishingly, Ali Musa's daughter, Almaz, became a Christian and started attending our Bible study. She genuinely believed her father to be a good person. She couldn't accept he was a cruel man. Ali Musa remained in post only a few months, before being replaced by another cruel governor. And so it continued.

The next governor, Gezaheign Werku stated in a speech that he would go house-to-house and hunt down this newcomer religion. He meant us. He did, indeed, put dozens of Christians in prison, including many I had discipled.

Gezaheign was a former army corporal, short, strongly built and utterly expressionless. I received my graduation certificate from him in 1989, (see his picture) and as I took it from his hand I looked into his eyes. I could see no humanity in him. Gezaheign later tried to flee the country with a sack of money he'd stolen from a bank. Before heading for the border, he went to the prison to kill the prisoners. Some Christians there survived the massacre. Before he could escape, he was surrounded by fighters. Rather than surrender to them, he killed his 18-year-old son and took his own life.

Gezaheign's predecessor, Ali Musa, also later committed suicide.

So much cruelty. The Eritrea I'd been born and raised in was a very conservative society and highly religious. People would always be encouraged to do some act of kindness, to give something to a beggar. If you saw someone who was hurting, you were expected to support them. If you saw a man hitting a girl, you would go over and try to stop him. The whole community had agreed to support one another. Suffering would not be tolerated.

But this government had been indoctrinated by Chinese Communism. The President had gone to China in his early 20s and was trained under Mao in the late 60s. He picked up the notion of treating people brutally, and he brought that brutality into his army and his political leaders. So we began to see something unimaginable.

In our culture, we respected a priest. If you saw a priest, you wouldn't just pass by; you would stop and kiss his hand or kiss his cross. But when this new breed of soldiers saw a priest, they would mock him, beat him, arrest him, and send him to prison. This was unnatural for us.

They completely destroyed our culture. And after that, they could get away with anything, however barbaric. In Eritrea, humanity was dying. We no longer saw ourselves as human beings.

When I pray for those who lead Eritrea, I pray for a miracle. It is only a miracle that can save us now. I used to pray for some sort of change, but not now. I believe it will take a whole new generation to bring about change. I pray that God will do something unthinkable, like when the Berlin Wall fell.

The fall of the Wall was unimaginable because Communism was so deeply rooted in East Germany. And nobody expected those roots to be pulled overnight. But in Germany the church was praying and tens of thousands gathered at the Wall, so the soldiers couldn't shoot. And that was the hand of God. And I pray for the same thing in Eritrea. I pray for a miracle, like the resurrection of Jesus, for out of darkness to come hope; for something to happen that I cannot begin to imagine.

14

ASMARA UNDER FIRE

My medical school years were some of the happiest in my life. The fellowship was good and we cared for one another. We discipled each other to become strong in our faith. We were like a family. And the connections I made then have remained to this day. We were able to get alongside others too, which opened up a way to share our faith. I learned that external pressures are not as important as the internal decisions we make and the faith in God that we exercise.

One Bible verse continued to be important for me during those years: 'Little children, you are from God and have overcome them, for he who is in you is greater than he who is in the world.' (1 John 4:4). People often asked me why I appeared so happy and relaxed. The answer was simple: because of Jesus. I always felt that the Lord and his heavenly hosts were on my side.

The threat of persecution was undiminished. The authorities used the media to defame Christians at every opportunity. They attacked us in youth groups and at every gathering. They made Christians out to be monsters, traitors, and spies of the CIA. The government controlled all the media, and used it to promote Communism, Marxism, Leninism and atheism. And only the Christians stood in their way. We would not be silent.

The government had given evil men the power and authority to do whatever they liked. Evil is the wilful abuse of power.

And our governors were men who had no regard for the wellbeing of others, who destroyed families and the young, who took it upon themselves to torture, kill and destroy. One governor, Melaku Tefera, hanged a ten-year-old boy in the market for stealing a sheep. He went on to murder hundreds of young people.

Despite the persecution, the numbers in our Lutheran church had risen to more than 100. Other Christian groups started home cell churches, drawing the anger of the authorities who rounded up and arrested people in the city.

They asked some if they'd converted to Christ as a result of my preaching, as by now I had something of a reputation. But I also had a measure of protection, as an edict from the Ethiopian President prohibited local authorities from interfering within the grounds of universities. So, the authorities regularly spied on me, to try to catch me preaching in the town. Had they succeeded, they would have arrested me there and then.

I completed my final exams successfully. I'd passed all my years and achieved B grades across the board, with one A and one C.

In the summer I returned to Eritrea – my first visit home since my mother's death. I was used to her greeting me and hugging me – and knew that wouldn't happen this time. As the taxi came closer to my family home the tears fell uncontrollably down my cheeks. All I could see was my mother opening the door, running to me and embracing me. And that was never going to happen again.

I graduated in 1989 and was given a one-year internship at the hospital in Gonder where I'd studied. Everything is arranged when you study at university: your food and accommodation are all provided. But during the internship you have to start paying! The wage was decent enough, but I had to find money for the first month. And while I was praying about this, my pastor called me and told me the church had decided to give me a sum of money. It was enough to cover my flight back to Gonder, taxi costs and food for one month.

I was less active in the underground church during my year of internship, I wanted to hand over the leadership to others, as I knew I'd be leaving soon. But I continued to preach in the Lutheran church.

After internship I was assigned a post by the Minister of Health. Thankfully I was sent to Asmara to work in an eye hospital. But all doctors were required to do some service in the military hospital, and after just two months I was reassigned.

The military hospital was good and clean, and the nurses highly skilled. Asmara was still under Ethiopian control. All the soldiers were Ethiopian and viewed us with suspicion. You can't tell Ethiopians and Eritreans apart by looking at them, but you can tell where they're from by their accent. Whenever I asked a question, they refused to answer. If I asked a wounded soldier where he'd come from, he wouldn't tell me.

One morning, at about 4am, a truck load of some 40 casualties arrived. The only questions I was allowed to ask were about their wounds. I was the only doctor on the night shift. I had to screen all the casualties and send on those with severe chest wounds and head injuries to specialised hospitals. The rest I had to deal with myself.

Asmara Expo had been turned into a makeshift hospital. It was supposed to treat 2,000 wounded soldiers, with only two doctors. On one sunny day, I went outside for lunch with the Ethiopian officers and medical workers, when we heard shooting. Within moments, everyone had disappeared. All the army officers had fled. Somehow, I could tell the shooting was not an immediate threat, so I stayed put. When the soldiers returned, they found me where they'd left me. A captain asked: 'Aren't you scared? All of us are scared, that's why we're running.'

I replied: 'Where could I go?' It turned out the shooting we'd heard was a Colonel being shot in the back by his own bodyguard with an AK47.

I heard on the news that the Eritrean freedom fighters had captured the port of Massawa, about 70 miles from Asmara. Massawa was on a plain and highly defended. Many tanks were dug in to defend that long approach. That it would be possible for lightly armoured soldiers to get through that ring of steel seemed inconceivable.

But the Eritreans took Massawa, unit by unit. And they sent many soldiers fleeing in confusion. The defending tanks were unable to fire for fear of hitting their own retreating army. The Eritreans were prevented from taking Massawa from the land, because burning tanks had blocked the narrow bridge. In the end, they attacked the port from the sea, killing many civilians.

The moment I heard the news, I returned to the hospital. I knew we would soon be facing many more casualties. Our hospital was next in line from Massawa.

Within two or three days every bed was filled with 2,000 casualties. The Ethiopians were struggling to retake the port and by now the Eritrean fighters controlled the road all the way from Asmara.

Many wounded soldiers died of septicaemia and if we saw any with self-inflicted wounds we were supposed to report them. Had we done so they would have been executed. I refused to report them. I told the commander, 'These are my patients. It is my job to treat their wounds.'

One day Etsegenet, the Ethiopian doctor working alongside me, came in smiling: 'Thirty-five have been executed!' she beamed. Another time, two planes crashed in Massawa. One had been fired on and exploded, taking down its escort plane. Both crashed, killing all the pilots. Etsegenet was sad: 'We lost two planes!' she lamented.

'What about the pilots?' I asked. Etsegenet was forever accusing me of being unpatriotic. Her husband, a captain, was captured in Northern Ethiopia, fighting the Tigrean rebels.

By now, Asmara was encircled and in range of EPLF artillery. They were shelling Asmara from outside. All our food and fuel had to be flown in by plane from Ethiopia. The airlift went on for more than a year from February 1990 to May 1991. Ethiopian passenger jets, Boeings and Soviet-era Antonovs were vying to bring in essential supplies for civilians and the military. And whenever the flights tried to land, the EPLF did their best to shoot them down – they managed to disable one cargo plane.

The war was drawing to a close and Asmara had become the centre of the conflict.

My ticket out – for the time being – came when I was referred to an eye doctor in Addis Ababa, due to the effect of diabetes on my eyesight.

While I was in the Ethiopian capital I was offered a job in a children's health centre. It was there I heard the news that Eritrean fighters had finally taken Asmara – as expected. But what was unexpected is that they hadn't stopped there. In collaboration with Tigrayan fighters they began chasing President Mengistu's forces out of the country. Many Ethiopian soldiers surrendered.

By now, I was leading several fellowships in Addis, was chairman of the Ethiopian medical fellowship; and was coordinating home Bible studies, prayer groups and conferences. I was also coordinating the national intercessory movement. Its main aim was to pray for peace and reconciliation, as there was ongoing ethnic tension and Christians were not exempt from that. We met every Friday evening, a group of about 30 from different regions of Ethiopia. I was the only Eritrean, and I was the leader, which was a little uncomfortable. Most of those I was involved with were Ethiopians.

Ethiopia is a land of more than 80 ethnic groups, with constant tension between them. Many Ethiopians are Orthodox Christians, while about a third are Muslim. Those I was living with were angry, having fought to keep Eritrea as part of

Ethiopia. Without Eritrea, Ethiopia no longer had access to the sea. So while the Ethiopians were crying, the Eritreans were celebrating. It was awkward.

There was no telephone access, so I often had no idea what was happening. What I did know was that Asmara was flooded with missiles, tanks and weapons. And what I feared was that if the Ethiopian army determined to fight on there would be a bloodbath – and my family were all in Eritrea.

Many feared a new religious or ethnic conflict could flare up at any time. People were becoming increasingly nationalistic and tribalistic. Out intercessory group had its work cut out. Even in the church, people were talking against one another. I urged them: 'Please don't pray according to what you hear on the news. We need to seek the face of God. What is God's plan for Ethiopia?'

Our main prayers were to seek God's will and for the Church to follow the Lord. We wanted to bring unity. We wanted the church to stay neutral and keep out of tribal politics, which would only destroy it. God gave me favour – everybody was coming to these prayer meetings and the Church at that time was kept outside the conflict.

Before long the war followed me to Addis Ababa, which fell to the Tigrayan and Eritrean fighters. When they captured the city it could have led to civil war. But our intercessory group prayed against it and there was a peaceful transition. Mercifully, the Ethiopian army surrendered.

15

ALONG CAME ALEM

When independence for Eritrea was finally declared I had no idea what to do, in terms of future employment. I'd planned to continue living in Ethiopia. I was working in a good hospital. I enjoyed my job and my ministry in the church and was still leading the national intercessory group.

The law forbade us from meeting in private houses for religious purposes, so our prayer meetings had to be held in secret, in the home of an aunt, Kidisti. Her husband, General Isaias, was my mother's cousin. He was executed by President Mengistu for working for the Ethiopian emperor Haile Selassie. General Isaias was killed by the military junta along with 60 ministers and military commanders. They also executed his daughter. After this, Kidisti became a committed Christian and allowed several Christian fellowships to meet at her house in Addis Ababa.

One evening my aunt invited a young woman by the name of Alemtsehay to join us. She was tall, good-looking, with attractive brown eyes and a small, gentle smile. Alemtsehay worked in the National Statistics Office and became a believing Christian about eight years earlier, although she was from a church-going background.

We chatted after the meeting and I walked Alemtsehay to the taxi. I saw her the following Sunday at church, but she had a young man with her, a university lecturer from Asmara. And the next time she came, the man came with her. So that was that.

But that didn't stop my meddling aunt from persisting with her matchmaking. Aunt Kidisti found out this young man was actually Alemtsehay's cousin. So my aunt had a word. She told Alemtsehay: 'My relative has been asking about you. He wants you to call him.'

Aunt Kidisti had planted the seed and Alemtsehay watered it. She rang. We met for a coffee in the garden of the swish Wabisheble Hotel in Addis Ababa. We talked about our faith and the things we had in common. When I'd thought she was engaged, I hadn't paid much attention. But now I knew better, my interest perked up. And Alemtsehay knew it. It was early days, but the attraction was there, at least on my part. I was seeing this woman in a new light. Alemtsehay, though – Alem for short – seemed hesitant.

In June 1992 she went to London for two month's training in demographics. Over those two months, she simply disappeared without trace. She never wrote a word, and I began to wonder whether she would ever be coming back. Then the phone rang. It was Alem, just back from London. Bad timing. My bags were packed, and I was about to head off to the airport to fly to Asmara. A German intercessory group had called me over to join them there. 'I'm sorry,' I said. I'll be back in a month.' Alem said nothing.

That month passed, and we began seeing one another at prayer meetings and church, and in the garden of that swish hotel just two bus stops from her house. We were seeing one another regularly. And it was at the Wabisheble Hotel that I asked her, 'Do you love me?'

She replied: 'I don't hate you...'

Not a smile. Nothing. Alem was always serious when she talked. And this was no exception. She was completely straight faced. But by then, I had started to study this girl. And I had an idea what she meant. What she *really* meant – I hoped – was, 'I love you… but just wait.'

I'm a patient man, so I waited. And Alem began to call more often. She wanted to see me every evening. And most evenings we ate together, but still we never talked about our relationship. Which I found frustrating, because when I'd asked her, 'Do you love me?' I was ready to take things further.

But Alem just left me hanging. So I tried again: 'Do you love me?'

She replied: 'I like you.' Still no smile.

'Why don't you say I love you?' I pressed. 'Why do you only say I like you?'

'It's too early. I need a bit of time.'

Like I said, I'm a patient man, and I didn't want to put her under pressure. Eritrean girls seem to need to be begged and expect men to chase them. But I was not like that. And that surprised her.

Gradually we began to talk more about our relationship and finally we discussed getting married. But there was a problem.

Alem was constantly going to church – I mean constantly. And she was always asking the prophets in her church to pray for her. One warned her, 'This man is not what you expect. Don't get your hopes up.' Another priest also disapproved of me. And he was a Lutheran.

I asked her: 'Why do you keep going to other people? It's like going to a witch to tell your fortune. Look at me,' I said to her. 'How would you feel living for the rest of your life with me? Do you like me or not?'

'Has God spoken to you?' she asked.

'No,' I replied. 'I love you. That is enough.' And, indeed, that was enough for me.

Finally, at last, Alem smiled.

Despite all the prophets who'd done their best to discourage her, Alem said God had spoken to her. As she'd been worshipping

Dr Berhane with his mother and father, sister Bsrat, nephew Mulubrhan and cousin Gedeon. They were also living with his parents. This picture was taken in the early 1980s.

In my parents house in Asmara.

Dr Berhane sitting outside his house in Gonder city with a hymn book. This is during his internship.

Dr Berhane's graduation, receiving his certificate from the Governor. He was a very cruel person sent a lot of Christian to prison and killed many political prisoners.

Dr Berhane's graduation in 1989 with his father next to him.

Graduation Day in Gonder.

*Ethiopian medical doctors fellowship in early 1990s.
Dr Berhane was the elected chairman.*

Berhane and Alem's wedding day, January 24th 1993

In Ghana with missionary Ed Clotz.

Dr Berhane's wife Alem and his daughter Hermon 1996 at home in Asmara, Eritrea.

Dr Berhane with members of a new village church in western Eritrea. This is in the late 1990s.

My ordination party with family and friends, June 2008.

Dr Berhane with Twen in Germany 2024. Twen served 16 years in Eritrean prisons. She was released in 2021.

Dr Berhane with Wisdom, in the north of England 2024. Wisdom's father Luul served 14 years in prison in Eritrea for his faith in Jesus. She is 15 years' old and was reunited with him in October 2023 through the work of Release Eritrea.

in church, a man said, 'There is a girl at the back who is thanking God with her arms raised.' He added: 'God is going to bless you in the next two weeks.' And within those two weeks Alem had met me.

And from that time on, we started planning our wedding. We had come to an understanding.

In our culture, most marriages are arranged. Ours was an exception – unless you count my meddling aunt.

I asked Alem if she wanted to wait, or would prefer to marry soon. She said, 'Soon.' So I knew it must be love.

When we express love in our culture, we don't say so explicitly. We hint. I never gave Alem flowers, but I gave her a Bible. A beautiful, blue leather-bound King James Bible with bright gold edges.

Rather like me, Alem doesn't express her emotions. She kept her distance, so sometimes I worried if she truly loved me or not. But deep down, I knew.

We began planning our wedding for January 1993. This was only some six months after we'd met. Some of our friends thought it too soon, but we were in love and the decision felt right. So we began looking for a church.

Kale Hiwot said we would have to wait six months and attend marriage classes. But we didn't want to wait that long. I was 37 and Alem was 35. We knew our minds and we were ready.

Alem's parents were Eritrean and were happy that I was Eritrean too, and a Christian minister. Alem was also from a Lutheran background, so we married in her local Lutheran church, Mekene Yesus, in Addis Ababa.

My father and sister came from Asmara, as did Tadesse, my brother, who was a commercial driver in Saudi Arabia. It was a wonderful family gathering, and a large one, too! We invited 400, many of whom were doctors from the medical fellowship.

In the early morning we went to Alem's house, where there was singing and preaching, and we ate together. Then in the afternoon we went to the Lutheran church for our wedding service, followed by refreshments in the church courtyard. The day had started sunny, but it began to rain. And as the guests streamed to their cars, the street boys poured into the park to finish off the picnic.

I was pleased and relieved. I was with the woman I loved. Our love had grown stronger the longer we were together. What had drawn me to Alem was her beauty, both within and without. She was always caring, always constant, and never up and down in her emotions.

We spent a two-week honeymoon around the Rift Valley lakes in Ethiopia. And we followed this with a six-week stay at my uncle's house in February. Then we headed off to Germany for a speaking tour of churches that took in Berlin, Frankfurt and Dresden. The mountains near Dresden took our breath away.

We travelled to the beautiful city of Prague and were delighted with its mechanical clock and bridge. People were playing flutes on the street and I bought myself a recorder. Then we went to Holland, where we stayed with my sister Mebrat. We were combining ministry with times of rest.

Alem was happy to watch me minister to others. And this extended break gave me more time to get to know my new wife. Whenever we clashed it was usually short-lived and we grew to appreciate one another more and more.

When we returned, we came to live with Alem's mother in Addis. This was far from ideal, as Alem was posted to work in the statistics office in Asmara more than 700 miles away. She stayed with my family there, while I worked in Addis at Amanuel Psychiatric Hospital. I'd been saving up my annual leave, and after a month, I went to join her. And there I decided to stay. I quit my old job and found myself back in Asmara.

16

UNDER GOD'S CURSE?

Thirty years of war had destroyed most of Eritrea's infrastructure. In most cities only Orthodox churches and mosques survived. There were no Evangelical churches.

I wanted to continue my medical career and combine that with church ministry. Those intentions came together in a vision for developing medical facilities for small towns via a mobile clinic. Along with that was a county-wide mission, focusing on an unreached people group, most of whom were Muslims. If I could combine my medical skills with my ministry experience in Ethiopia, I believed I could accomplish this vision, if I had the help of the church's wider ministry. But my vision for a mobile clinic was thwarted – the government wouldn't allow it.

My church (Kale Hiwot) is known for its holistic approach to ministry. The church ran schools and an orphanage but was also involved in well-drilling and the construction of roads and micro-dams. The church supported farmers by terracing hillsides and planting trees. My vision was for the church to retain this holistic approach – but to be more proactive when it came to evangelism and church planting.

Eventually I was offered a job upgrading hospitals in Eritrea. We had a contract with a Swedish charity that was sending medical supplies and hospital equipment. My job was to decide which hospitals to supply. It was good as far as it went, but I still had a yearning to combine health care with Christian ministry.

In 1994 Uganda was in the grip of the AIDS epidemic. I was invited to the capital, Kampala, for a conference. Uganda was the world epicentre for HIV at the time. Entire communities had been wiped out.

I visited many AIDS sufferers in their homes, all of whom had simply been left to die. The social stigma of AIDS was unimaginable, so people had little support from either their communities or the church. The conference discussed prevention and care, as back then there was still no effective treatment for AIDS. At the time I remember wondering what Jesus would do in a situation like this. I thought of Jesus ministering to the lepers, the woman suffering from bleeding, the demon-possessed, the blind, the mute and the lame. I wanted to be like Jesus and to help the marginalised, the poor and those despised even by their own families. My stay in Kampala was challenging and was to have an impact on my future ministry.

When Jesus looked on the crowd, he had compassion on them. He recognised that they had come far, were tired and needed something to eat. It convinced me that Christian ministry is far more than just preaching.

Christians believed these AIDS patients were under God's curse. They were being punished by God for their infidelity. But I didn't see it that way. Many of these HIV victims were housewives. They caught this disease from their husbands. And I didn't want to judge either them or their spouses.

No-one who had been healed by Jesus was perfect. All of them were sinners – without exception. But Jesus treated them as friends. He took time to speak to the Samaritan woman. It was Jesus' ministry on health that became my role model. I saw Jesus as ministering to the whole person, not just getting souls to heaven. That Samaritan woman could not find love. She had been dumped many times. And Jesus wanted to fix that. He spoke to her about relationship. In the Baptist Church where I'd grown up, we'd focused on truth, but neglected the compassion, which was so essential if we're ever to connect with the poor and the needy.

In my sermons, I always preached from the gospels. How should we live in this world? How should we put our faith into practise? How could we provide love, generosity and care? And I always found Jesus to be the best example. The AIDS patients in Uganda were desperate for love, but nobody would come close enough to love them, because they were scared of catching AIDs. I wondered: where is the Church of Uganda? The Church needs to care for them. A few Christians were, but not enough. Most of the carers came from other parts of the world, but not from Uganda.

HIV was nothing short of an epidemic. And that was partly because of the tradition in Uganda. If the husband died, the brother inherited the wife. The tradition of wife sharing, meant that HIV was widely sexually transmitted. It destroyed some neighbourhoods entirely.

By the time people started to ask, why did this happen to me it was already too late. Some in the church were teaching that if these people could not abstain, then let them die. Yes, the church needed to teach fidelity and abstinence, but those who failed still needed to take protection so they would not infect their wives. But the church could not bring itself to accept that. I knew the church had to find a way to offer correction without condemnation, that we had to show them compassion.

When I returned to Asmara my church appointed me to lead its spiritual ministry department. Our church had around 200 members in Asmara and another 50 or so scattered around other towns. Immediately I set about training young people in evangelism. I planned to train 30 for three weeks and send them out to evangelise for three months. We would pay for their transportation and living costs, but they would get no salary. But even without the expense of paying them, I still had no funds.

At that time Billy Graham's son Franklin, who was CEO of Samaritan's Purse, came to visit projects that his organisation was funding. Over a meal, I shared my vision. He asked me how much it would cost, and I said $10,500. He promptly wrote out a cheque for the full amount.

The recruiting and training went well. We sent our people out two by two to about a dozen towns. After about three months all came back and most wanted to carry on. I was given additional funding. They began to plant churches. After just one year our church membership had almost doubled to more than 400. And over the next four years, this increased to 1,000. Many of those young people later became pastors and some are still involved in ministry all over the world.

Numbers continued to grow, along with the persecution. And we continued to plant churches. Then in 1998, war broke out again with Ethiopia. There was a border dispute over the village of Badme. Eritrea said the village belonged to us and occupied it by force. The Ethiopians fought back and pushed the Eritreans out.

The Tigrayans had fought with Eritrea in the previous war. This time they were fighting against us. They penetrated hundreds of kilometres into Eritrea and were getting close to the capital, Asmara, when the United Nations told them to back off.

The Tigrayans retreated but held on to that border town. The UN decided the town should be handed back to Eritrea but the Ethiopians refused. The village of Badme has continued to be a flashpoint.

And the government, looking for a scapegoat, blamed the Christians for losing the war. They accused us of pledging our allegiance to heaven or the West, and instead of praying, we should be fighting for our country.

They had another problem with Christians, too. And that was our compassion. In the military, when they train the soldiers, they train them to be killing machines. If a man is asked to kill his mother, he has to obey. If he is asked to kill his brother, he has to do it.

One of the fighters told his story. He'd been passing his own village and heard someone shouting from the rooftops that there was to be a funeral tomorrow – his mother's. So he told his commander. And his commander said, 'Shut up. You don't have a mother.' The grieving soldier was not even allowed to visit his father.

If the soldiers cry, the punishment will be harsh. They are raising them to be brutal. And now we see even among some Christians in that country a new and brutal type of Christianity, Christians who are preaching violence, who admire the President for being anointed by God to be strong, and who deny he has committed any crimes.

And so the persecution intensified.

One of our evangelists, Philipos, was called up for national service. He didn't hesitate to perform his national duty. There were others, such as Jehovah's Witnesses, who were conscientious objectors, but Evangelicals like Philipos were usually willing to fight. Philipos was bold. He'd been pastoring a church when they took him for military service, and he'd been serving in the army on the frontline.

I was at the church office in Asmara, when Philipos walked in in military fatigues, straight from the field. He was well built and very strong. He was tall and always walked upright. His skin was dark and his hair thick and straight. Philipos was an evangelist from the church I'd led in Eritrea. I loved him like a son. We took our meals together and I'd given him my bicycle, so he could visit people. Philipos had been new in the faith, but he grew quickly. Today, he looked worried.

He said they'd arrested and detained him for three days, beat him, then released him. His commander had warned him about his faith. Philipos was a quiet man, but when the commander ordered him to stop worshipping and preaching he refused.

Philipos told me, 'I'm not afraid, Berhane. My commander is a soldier, and I am a soldier.' But concern was written on his face.

We talked for only ten minutes. Then we stood together and shook hands. I hoped to see him again, but later heard that Philipos had disappeared.

Soldiers were forbidden from reading the Bible, praying or sharing their faith. Philipos was a man full of confidence. And when the government sees a man full of confidence, they want to break him. They want to rule by fear. It is fearful people who seek to rule by fear. And their fear was that Christians would establish their own power base in opposition.

By then the EPLF were in control. They told Philipos' mother that her son had been killed in action. But later, my relative told me he had met someone who had witnessed his execution. This had been carried out in public.

Philipos was a Christian martyr, the first of a new wave of martyrs in Eritrea.

These men and women were my friends. I really loved them. And I have never forgotten them. I campaign for them always and for the release of those behind bars. But I still feel guilty for sending them out as sheep to the wolves.

And then I remind myself that it was not I who was sending them. It was Jesus. They were responding to His calling.

In war, soldiers are recruited and sent to the frontline, where some, inevitably, will be killed. Why should our spiritual warfare be any different?

What is different for us is that death is not the end. It is only the beginning.

17

CHANGING LIVES

It was two years into our marriage and Alem and I wanted to start a family. It was getting late in life for us to have a child, and we were beginning to worry. We'd been praying and the church was praying for us. I was particularly concerned for my wife. In our culture it's the wife who gets the blame if a couple fail to produce children.

Then, after a bout of illness, Alem had a test and was found to be pregnant. We were so happy! But the pregnancy was difficult for Alem. She was sick throughout and struggled to eat. And when she did eat, she couldn't keep her food down. We were beginning to wonder whether she would be able to keep going right to the end. When the time came, her labour lasted for days and her strength was failing. She had to be induced.

In my country, fathers are not permitted to be present at the birth. Even though I was a doctor and have worked in a maternity hospital, they still wouldn't allow me in. All I could do was to stand outside the door, listening, waiting and hoping for the sound of a crying baby. But there was nothing. With me was my friend, a paediatrician who worked at the hospital.

And then a nurse came out and said: 'Your wife has survived – but the baby has died.'

I said, 'What?' I swung open the door and pushed my friend inside. I was still not allowed in. They told me the baby was neither crying nor breathing. But the paediatrician gave her suction and some injections and then – thank God – she started to cry.

And at that cry began one of the happiest days of my life – I was overwhelmed with joy. We named our baby daughter Hermon. The name came from Mt Hermon in Israel, which is described in Psalm 133 as a mount of blessing. I had a friend called Hermon because everybody liked him. And our daughter Hermon was God's blessing to our family.

Straight away I picked up Hermon and held her. She was a healthy 3.3kg. Beautiful, innocent, and with such lovely soft skin – although as a newborn she looked every bit as wrinkled as my aged aunts.

Alem was exhausted, and because she'd been unable to hold her food, she was starving and couldn't produce milk for the baby. So we had to feed Hermon with formula milk. I loved my new daughter so much; I was always making excuses to come home from work to see her!

Church was also thriving. I was the director for spiritual ministries, in charge of pastors, evangelists, church planting, training and the Bible school. It was a big job. It seemed that new members were being added every day and new churches planted in every corner of the country.

We had about 1,200 members in 14 churches and more workers than ever. We had some 38 pastors and more than 200 development workers. Some 400 people attended my own church in Asmara. We were distributing food, grain and oil to the needy, and we'd built the church under the noses of the government to look like a grain store. They never inspected it. Outside it was a warehouse, surrounded by storage containers full of medical and farm equipment, but inside it was a church.

God continued to provide the finances we needed. We were busy purchasing houses for the church and organising the construction of new schools in Muslim-majority towns.

God was good, and gave me favour with a number of small-town mayors, governors and community leaders, including the Muslims who we were helping. They saw Evangelicals as less of a threat than the Orthodox, because we were in a minority. And like the Muslims, we didn't drink alcohol, so we had something in common.

We had only a few Muslim converts, and those who accepted the gospel kept a low profile. We experienced no serious hostility from the Muslims. Even when we built schools, they could see the benefit of what we were building for the community.

In fact, we had more of a problem with the Orthodox than the Muslims. They continued to call us newcomers, who were following the religion of the West. They accused us of being anti-Mary, of refusing to venerate their saints. Family members who were Orthodox sometimes refused to come to weddings. And if there was a funeral, the Orthodox would sometimes prevent us from burying our dead in the graveyard.

I was invited to speak at a conference in a small town. The Orthodox priest gathered hundreds of villagers who began to throw stones at the church. We were showered with them. One stone came through the window and hit my shoulder. We had to call the police. I don't know what would have happened had the police not arrived. Some of these people were real extremists, who didn't care whether we lived or died. In Ethiopia, a similar group plucked out the eyes of a young girl who was about to get married. They said it was because she was a follower of this new religion.

Many who called themselves Orthodox had been taught little about their faith and seldom went to church. Yet if you asked them their religion, they would say Orthodox. Most had a limited understanding of their religion and would not have been able to tell you what they believed. When the priests lead mass they use a different language from the ordinary people. Their religion was just part of their culture. But things were beginning to change. And because of the persecution we were more inclined to respect one another's differences.

There are problems with all our traditions, including my own. I've yet to find a church that is perfect. What really matters is salvation through Christ. I've never asked anyone to change their church. When I was evangelising and someone would say they went to the Orthodox church, I would say, 'Okay, no problem. But you need to read the Bible. You need a personal connection with Jesus.'

I will never insult another person's faith. What I look for is common ground. There are many Orthodox priests in prison today because they preach the gospel. And we are working together with them. They in turn were often persecuted by the hardliners and traditionalists in their church for choosing to preach in a language the people could understand. These priests were considered modernists and many were kicked out of the church. Most our own church members had come from that tradition, and once the ordinary Orthodox believers got to know us, they softened their hearts and came to like us.

There is a word of scripture that always sticks in my heart: Love your neighbour as yourself. My neighbour could be Orthodox. So my first approach is to love them, to care for them, and to be available when they need me. And I try to explain that I'm doing this because of Jesus, so they can know Jesus more. If we tell them Jesus is love, but then insult them, how can they see His love? Jesus drew followers from many different backgrounds, but he met their needs. He put his words and his love into action.

For me, that also meant working on the development side of the church in charge of medical projects. I was providing medical equipment to hospitals and centres for people going through rehabilitation after the war. My church was donating equipment and resources free of charge to government hospitals.

The government wasn't particularly happy with this, as they didn't want our church to have any impact or influence on

Eritrean society. Several times health officials told me to stop importing medical supplies from Sweden. We were bringing in refurbished beds, mattresses, dental chairs and laboratory equipment. All of it was like new. And the authorities needed every bit of it, but because they didn't want the church to be seen to be helping the community, they tried to prevent it.

All that changed when war broke out again with Ethiopia. The army had nothing: no beds, no wheelchairs, no bandages. So the Ministry of Defence sent me a letter, asking us to get this equipment. And they gave me permission to bring wheelchairs and crutches into the army camps. Our favour increased. Suddenly, those who opposed us became our friends.

We had also established a large farm, of about 200 hectares. The soil was dark and fertile and began to generate funds to support our orphanage and some of the pastors. Sadly, that farm was later confiscated by the government.

Despite the hard-liners in the government, we had little trouble from the local authorities. Most of the hostility towards the church came right from the top. But our relations with officials varied from place to place.

In one town, neighbours complained about a noisy all-night prayer meeting, and the police were called out. They arrested our church members and beat some of them badly.

I drove straight to the police station and asked to speak to the commander. To begin with he was angry and defensive. I asked him whether he'd arrested the Christians because of an order from the top. 'If it came from the top, I will go to the top,' I insisted. But the commander said he'd given the order to carry out the arrests.

Many of the girls had been beaten and covered with bruises. So I gently challenged him: 'How can you do that to girls? The police are supposed to know how to behave.' I said I would report him to his superiors.

He replied: 'You don't need to do that. Why don't we just agree?' His officers had been called in after neighbours complained about a disturbance. They had a point. The neighbours accused the Christians of shouting in the middle of the night at the prayer meeting.

So we came to an agreement. After eight in the evening the Christians would either meet quietly or not at all, and there should be no further worship meetings after 8pm. It seemed a reasonable compromise, and the police commander released the Christians.

But the church was angry with me. They wanted to assert their right to hold all-night prayer meetings. So I had to explain that this was not an official church building, just a rented house in the middle of the neighbourhood. We wanted to be good neighbours, I said, but if your neighbours are angry, how can you share the gospel with them? The beating had been excessive and there was no need to send our members to prison, but our members should have been more considerate towards their neighbours. That's not compromising our freedom or the gospel – that's wisdom.

But of all the ministries I was involved in at that time the most successful was the microcredit business. Devora's husband left her after she converted to Christ. She was in her mid-thirties and a mother of four, and a fifth child was on the way. Devora was strong in her faith, but was struggling to feed her children and often in tears. She would turn up at the church office for anything we could give her. I used to give her something from the little fund Alem and I kept for the needy. But we were taking care of everyone from that, and the money wouldn't stretch. So Alem pointed out that we needed to find a lasting solution.

The church began a micro-finance project. It was intended to help people like Devora start a business, but these people were often so poor that they used it to meet pressing immediate needs, such as buying food or furniture, paying the rent or servicing debt. The approach failed, and I was angry.

But my wife's auntie Yirga was working for the government in microcredit, and at the time Alem was employed as a project co-ordinator for World Vision. Between them, they had the expertise we needed. They could evaluate what we were doing and get it to work. So their advice was to look for people passionate about running their own businesses, to offer them training and put in place a team to support them. So we started over and hired Yirga to help run the microenterprise initiative.

Devora was the first beneficiary. We gave her a loan at a low rate of interest, and she started a poultry farm and made a real success of it. I visited her a couple of years later. By then, Devora was keeping 300 chickens and selling hundreds of eggs per day. She was well dressed and greeted me with a wonderful smile that told me she was happy and prosperous and had everything she needed. She was at last able to send her children to school, feed her family and pay the bills. And she had plans to double the number of chickens. Unfortunately, Devora ended up in prison for her faith in Christ, and remained there for many years.

Of the 100 women we funded, 90 per cent were successful. Some made peanut butter, others opened coffee shops or hair salons. And as they paid back their initial loans, we were able to offer more so they could grow their businesses. We continue to provide microcredit to this day, with the support of Release International and its sister organisation Voice of the Martyrs.

The scheme is simple but effective and has made a lasting difference. When people are persecuted the enemy always tells them, you are rubbish, you are nobody. But when they know that the whole world is praying for them, that the whole Christian community is on their side, they are greatly uplifted.

But by now, a perfect storm was brewing.

18

GATHERING STORM CLOUDS

After about six years into this work, I started to experience signs of burn out. There were challenges from the government, challenges within the church, and, with hindsight, personal challenges in the way I was conducting my ministry. At the time, I was unaware of just how those storm clouds were gathering.

The government was always trying to frustrate our work. They began arresting workers and shutting down rural churches. I could sense that a new wave of persecution was in the air and on the way. We had no clear idea how that would unfold, but the tell-tale signs were growing. The pressure was on. We had a limited window of opportunity and needed to use it to the full.

Back in the 70s, the freedom fighters had published a manifesto pledging their opposition to what they called western-sponsored religions. They mentioned by name Jehovah's Witnesses and Pentecostals. But when independence came in 1991, Communism had already collapsed in the Soviet Union. So we hoped the new government had reconsidered their opposition to religion, and changed their policies. And for a time, after they came to power, they never even mentioned religion.

To begin with, we were allowed to worship freely. The previous Ethiopian authorities had confiscated some of our church buildings, and we hoped the new government would return them, but they never did. Then, in 1997, the government began to shut down part of the church's development work. Their policy was far from clear.

We went to a village to show the *Jesus* film, a film that's been used around the world to tell the story of Jesus from the Bible simply and in many languages. It's been hugely successful in leading people to Christ. Many of the villagers had never watched a movie, and they turned out in large numbers to see the Jesus film. Furthermore, as far as we knew, there was no law to prevent us.

Just turning up with our generator and switching on the lights was an event in itself, as there was no electricity in the village. People were curious and came to find out what was happening. They watched the film and were very happy, and we distributed Bibles to those who came. But even though what we were doing was lawful, the government sued us and made us pay a substantial fine.

By now they were starting to shut some of our village churches and arrest our evangelists. I needed to determine their official policy on religion. So I went to the regional governor's office and asked him directly. But I didn't get a direct answer. He said, 'I knew what our policy was before independence, but I don't know now. If you want to find out, you'll have to go to the religious department.'

So I went to the capital, Asmara, and asked the head of the religious department directly: 'What's your policy?' He didn't want to answer. So I spelt it out. I told him we were planting churches everywhere in Eritrea and wanted to know whether evangelising was legal or illegal. And the commissioner, whose name was Dragon, said: 'I'm not going to tell you. You'll have to take it up with the local administrators.'

So why was the government shy about revealing their policy on religion? I believe they wanted to keep the policy secret, to avoid being labelled anti-religious in the West. They were getting a lot of financial aid and were determined to protect that. I went to many governors and police stations to try to clarify what we could and could not do. Then a friend warned me I was under surveillance and being followed. I needed to be careful.

The government was suspicious of anyone with an education or who could be considered an intellectual, so even my title Doctor was a kind of a crime. Some of the medical doctors, PhDs and pastors were in prison. The government was paranoid and feared we would report them to the international community.

The persecution was stepping up a gear. There was work to do. We had to be ready. I wanted to grab every opportunity and would work with anyone who was willing. The pressure was on.

A change in the church added to the challenge. Although we had many dedicated workers, we also had one or two troublemakers – and it only takes a handful to wreck a peaceful environment. There were some who saw themselves as prophets. And whenever you challenged them, they would tell you: 'We obey the spirit of God, rather than you.' There was no discussing the matter with these people. One man refused to go to the village where he'd been assigned. So I stopped his salary. And he sued me.

By now the church was huge, but for all that growth, we were still operating within limited resources, and we were never able to meet every need. We depended so much on workers who were willing to sacrifice themselves and their personal interests. Thankfully many were. But tiredness was creeping into some of the evangelists. Some were beginning to complain about their pay. Their fire was starting to dim.

Then the spiritual and development departments of the church were merged, and although I was allowed to keep my position as a spiritual director, I felt our work was being compromised. Before my arrival, our large development ministry was draining most of our church members who, instead of working in ministry, were working for development.

Ninety percent of our manpower was poured into this operation. We were building schools, had an orphanage and were constructing village dams. We were also planting trees and helping farmers with soil and water conservation. All that was good, but there was no longer the same spiritual input into this physical development. It was easier to get funding for practical development work because those holding the purse-strings respected our services as teachers or development workers.

Later, we put this right. When we were doing soil and water conservation, we would send an evangelist to gather the development workers. They would come together, and then invite people from the village, so that a church could be planted along with the work. That put the mission back on course, but at the time, I felt we were going off track.

With hindsight, I recognise that the biggest challenge was coming, not from church or government, but from within. I was struggling. I could feel my energy beginning to drain away. I was always planning, preparing, recruiting and training new people. It was becoming harder to persuade people to take on the work. And some of them began to refuse, spiritualising their reluctance by saying they had no vision to go to a particular place. All of this was taking its toll on me.

For six years now, I'd had no holidays. I was working from Monday to Sunday, travelling north, south, east, and west and doing all the development work, including negotiating with government officers. I took no time to sit and rest and recover. At weekends I was either preaching or visiting one of the newly planted churches. I was always busy but seemed unable to form a capable team around me that could share the workload.

Looking back, I can see I'd forgotten the importance of Sabbath, the importance of taking a rest. I can see I needed more personal discipline. I'd also failed to set up effective boundary lines between my personal life and the ministry. This affected everything, including time and money.

I would often use my own money for the ministry – until it ran out. If anyone said they were hungry and needed to feed their child, I would give them money from my back pocket. I would visit church after church, and often the church would not give me sufficient funds to cover my accommodation. I would also need to offer hospitality to those who came to visit me in the hotel, and that meant paying for them, which came from our own personal accounts.

But when it came to those I had recruited, I would give evangelists and pastors extra money for their own travel. This came out of church funds. And when I travelled overseas, such as to Germany to speak, every church would give me a donation. But I put every penny of that back into the church.

A missionary once came to my house and left me a plastic bag with $10,000. He told me I could use it for the church or I could use it for myself. The gift was anonymous. Nobody knew about it, but I passed it over to the church in full. If you lose your integrity, you lose everything. And I never wanted to give anyone the chance to accuse me of corruption.

Eventually, our personal funds became exhausted and we could no longer pay the rent on our house. I had to ask my father for a place to stay. And that pressure, inevitably, spilled over to Alem.

My wife was always generous, but she'd found herself out of work due to the government shutdown. Alem had been working for World Vision, but they closed it down along with other aid agencies, for fear they were spying on them. The government was so paranoid, they were suspicious of anything under the control of another nation. Whatever they couldn't control they would close down or destroy.

So Alem was out of a job. I was the only one being paid, and my salary was just not enough to cover my travel, our rent and our food. In the end, Alem, who seldom showed her feelings, said, 'No way! We just can't afford your travel!

You'll have to stop it.' But I wouldn't listen. I was not an easy person to live with.

What I have learned is that if you intend to last in this game, you must be disciplined – that's the message I would tell myself now. And that discipline has to be applied to your time as well as your money.

If I could roll back the years and grasp my younger self by my shoulders and tell myself a few choice words, I would say: 'Berhane, you must put a boundary on your finances and your time. And you must put boundaries on your relationship with church staff.' Because people would come to my house without notice and then expect to stay. It's part of our culture.

And in my memo to self, I would insist on being more open about my personal needs with those in responsibility.

It was the board of trustees who determined my salary and expenses, but I didn't want to negotiate with the board or waste time talking about my own interests. I didn't want them to think I was doing this for the money. I didn't want anyone getting the idea I was doing God's work for financial gain.

Perhaps I set the scene when they hired me. At the time we didn't discuss payment. I said, 'Don't worry, I'm not doing this for the money, I'm doing this for Jesus.' Looking back, I may have given the board the false impression that I was wealthy. I should have discussed all of this, especially with those close to me. But they didn't know. How could they? I never told them.

I suppose there is a message for the church in this, too. I considered it my responsibility to look after the needs of those who worked for me. I knew every evangelist and pastor and would always stand up for them. I gave them transportation money and helped them with their bills. I was looking out for them, but who was looking out for me?

The church considered me to be in charge and left me to it. My own bosses didn't ask how I was living or where. Not even when I had to move to my father's house.

I'm not condemning them, but we all have to do right by others. Today, I am a minister in the Church of England, and the picture is very different. They ask us if we're struggling to pay our bills. If so, we can apply for support. You're free to manage your own affairs or to seek help as you choose. So, the church is looking out for us, not just to see whether we are doing our job efficiently, but to see how we are living, and if we need help.

Perhaps it was pride that kept me silent. There were many people praising me in the church for all that I was doing. And although I didn't believe I needed that praise, it's human nature to prefer praise to criticism.

Whatever the reason, the fact is, I was burning out. And there were other warning signs, too.

I never got irritated with people, it's not part of my nature. I always try to keep my joy, and when I approach people, I always smile. But that smile had begun to disappear and I was getting irritated. I was starting to blame people for the way I felt. I always want to speak good of others. But now I was blaming the church, the evangelists and other people.

And that anger was building. I found myself shouting and screaming. It was a shock for those around me, and for me. I was also suffering from heartburn, which was a first. All the signs pointed clearly to stress, but to recognise those signs, you have to be willing to watch out for them.

As a doctor, my advice to my younger self back then would be simple: stop everything. You need rest.

Meanwhile, the pressure continued to build, from the government, within the church, and especially within myself. My profile in the country was higher than ever. And I was certain it was only a matter of time before I ended up back in prison. The storm clouds were gathering. And I was overwhelmed.

19

CALLED OUT AND CALLED UP

And just when it was all too much, I had an offer from Tearfund UK to come to Britain to study theology Christian theology and Islam.

Tearfund was one of our partners and was funding a number of projects. They were offering a study period of two years. It felt like God's timing. I was happy and relieved and accepted the offer without hesitation.

It was much more than just a way to ease the pressure. Around half the population of Eritrea were Muslims, and although we'd planted some churches in Muslim areas and had some converts, I felt we were not yet communicating the gospel to Muslims effectively. So I was intrigued at the prospect of studying Islam and thought this would help.

What I hadn't figured on was the outbreak of war, yet again. It was 1998 and border hostilities had erupted once again with Ethiopia. Nobody was allowed to leave the country. And to make matters worse I was served with my call-up papers for the Eritrean army.

I did not believe in this new war. I was set on leaving to study in the UK and I had suffered diabetes since my teens. Yet I knew it would be difficult to convince the authorities that I should not be conscripted.

I went to the relevant administrator with my certificate to

prove I was insulin-dependent and unfit for military service. But he took one look at it and handed it back. He would not accept it. 'You have been called to serve our army. You must report for military training! You can try and convince the doctors when you get there.'

But I knew there would be no proper doctors at the military training centre. It was in a remote part of the desert, and I'd heard of others with medical conditions who had died there. One was a neighbour, who also had diabetes. He'd been forced to join the army and had died during his first week of training. Others with asthma, epilepsy and various heart conditions had also died.

So I made up my mind to refuse. I told the administrator, 'I will not go. You can shoot me if you want, but you have no authority to send me.' He was furious and told me to leave his office.

I stood outside, angry and sad. But I knew military service could end my life on earth, war or no war. At that point, the administrator called me back and demanded to know why I had been so rude. I replied, 'I am not being rude. Why don't you listen to me? I have this serious condition which means I cannot do military training!' But he insisted the letter was not enough, it had to go further; it had to state specifically that I should be exempted from military service.

So I went straight to the hospital where I had worked. There was a meeting of the board that afternoon. The board met every two weeks, and ordinarily I might have had to wait for a hearing but, because of the urgency, they agreed to hear my case the same day. All the board members agreed in my favour and gave me a military exemption certificate which was finally accepted. It was God's intervention and I was thankful.

And so, because of this, I was able to get a visa to travel to the UK. My intention was to spend two years studying and then return. For the first three months I stayed with my brother

Bahta, at his house in Westbourne Park, West London. Bahta is five years older than me and had been working in Saudi Arabia. He fled from there during the Iraq war which ousted Saddam Husein and brought his wife and three children to the UK.

I arrived in England in September 1999, when the weather was getting colder and the skies darker. That was a struggle. As was English food. And the loneliness. In Eritrea, there would always be a knock at the door and people calling in for coffee, especially at weekends. Our church communities there are close. They're more like extended families. We would see each other all the time.

I'd been forced to travel to London on my own as my daughter had no passport. Hermon would have to stay with Alem until she could get one. I told Alem that when Hermon's passport arrived, they should go to Egypt first, where there would be a British Embassy with ambassadors. They did, remaining in Egypt for three weeks until they were given visas to join me in England.

There was no room for us all in my brother's house, so I moved to a bedsit in Kings Cross.

Alem and Hermon arrived four months after I left Eritrea, on January 1, 2000. It was the start of a new millennium and a new era for our family. I was 43 and Hermon was now four. It was crowded in that little bedsit but we were happy to be together, and it was altogether better than the accommodation I would have enjoyed as a conscript in Eritrea.

I studied at the London Bible school in Northwood, north London, known today as the London School of Theology. I took a one-year Diploma in Theology.

There were very few black students. At my first class, a student wrote on the board: 'Blacks are monkeys.' When the teacher came in she was furious – all these students were training to be pastors. I would also encounter prejudice later from higher up in the Church of England.

I was one of the oldest students and although my English vocabulary was good, I was finding it difficult to understand some English accents. Alem had good English. She'd studied for her master's degree in Australia.

I completed the Diploma and developed that into an MPhil. My focus was the expansion of Islam in Eritrea. The method used by the Muslims had been to adopt the local culture and then add Islamic elements, such as Muslim prayers. They were accepted because they addressed the needs of the people.

In 2001, I ventured back to Eritrea to do some research on Sufi shrines that had become places of pilgrimage. I was there for a month, but when I tried to return to the UK, the Eritrean government stopped me. Once again, they said: 'You can't leave the country – you have to serve in the army.'

I showed them the letter from the London Bible College stating I was undertaking research for the summer. But they didn't care. They wouldn't listen. So I produced my exemption certificate for diabetes. They said that would've been valid two years ago but not anymore.

I thought, 'What am I going to do? My wife and family are in England and I'm stuck here. How am I going to get back?' All these thoughts came rushing into my mind. I knew the same thing had happened to others who'd gone back to Eritrea for research. For some the only way out had been to get smuggled illegally across the border to Sudan.

At that time Eritrea had yet to close all the Evangelical churches and mine was still open. So they wrote a letter to the Religious Affairs department to confirm I was in the country to study. And the authorities finally allowed me to return the UK. It was a close call.

Back in London, we joined All Saints Church, Kings Cross, on the Barnsbury Estate. The church is closed now. It was a small Anglican congregation of 40 or 50. There was no vicar at the time: it was run by the people and they worshipped with a guitar. I liked it. The leader was very friendly and visited us. We became close friends and I was welcomed into the church.

However, back in Eritrea events were about to change dramatically – events that would also change the course of my life and ministry.

20

RELEASE ERITREA

By 2001, it was already clear which way the wind was blowing. The authorities were arresting many Christians in the villages and small towns, along with those they'd conscripted for military service. And in May 2002 the Eritrean government was starting to shut down churches, including my own. The only denominations they allowed to continue, because they felt they could control them, were the Orthodox, Catholic and Lutheran, along with Sunni Islam.

This was one of the saddest days of my life. It wasn't a total surprise: the harassment had been increasing and all the signs had been pointing in that direction. Senior church leaders were summoned and told a new law was being introduced, requiring every church to register with the government. And while that registration was being processed, those churches would have to stop meeting for worship. The pastors were angry, but most reluctantly accepted the situation.

I knew this was really serious. It would drive the Church underground, which would inevitably lead to arrests and suffering. This had happened during the Ethiopian Communist regime, and now history was repeating itself.

I was torn. Part of me wanted to go back to Eritrea there and then, as I was well experienced in leading an underground church and I felt I could help during this traumatic time –

but I still had a year of my studies to do.

The first Christians to be arrested were in the port town of Assab, close to the eastern border with Djibouti. There were about 100 of them. Most had been recruited into the military for national service. They were gathering at a house church which was raided. This was before the government closed the church and made such meetings illegal.

Most of the prisoners have since been released, although some died in prison. One was kept behind bars for 18 years.

Every prisoner would be beaten. They were told they could easily stop the beatings and get released – all they had to do was sign a piece of paper. This paper would say, 'I've committed a crime against my government and my people by following this illegal religion. I regret it and I will not do it again. If I am caught again, I'm willing to suffer any punishment, even to forfeit my life.'

Many would sign without even reading it because they were so afraid. And those who refused would endure the beatings and demands to renounce their faith indefinitely. The beatings would go on for years. And after all those years, many suffered nervous breakdowns. They lost their minds. In the end, 90 percent of the prisoners signed that paper.

The following year, 2003, news reached me that our pastor in Eritrea had been arrested. Our minister at All Saints Church, Kings Cross suggested holding a special week of prayer for the pastor and for the government to reverse its policy. I knew the persecution of Christians would not stop with registration – that was just the beginning – and I was desperate to go back to Eritrea and offer my support. But I knew I would probably be arrested, and if that happened, it would be my family who would suffer the most.

After the week of prayer our minister staged a five-day demonstration outside the Eritrean Embassy in London. It was just a ten-minute walk away. While it was heartening that

Christians in the UK wanted to show support for their fellow Christians, I felt I needed to draw the line at demonstrating outside the embassy. I was in the UK on a short-term student visa and still planned to return to Eritrea after my studies. If I joined that demonstration, I would probably never be able to go back.

I assumed that the government in Eritrea wouldn't know about me or be particularly concerned about me. But one Sunday an Eritrean lady turned up at church and the vicar introduced us. She was small and slim with long dark hair and gave her name as Nigisti. She said she was new to the country and looking for some support in studying English.

It was not unusual for Eritreans to seek one another out for help. And when she asked for my telephone number I gave it. She rang me that evening and asked what I was doing in the country, which church I'd belonged to in Eritrea and what the connection was between my church in the UK and my church back home. She also asked who was funding my studies. I explained it was a UK Christian charity called Tearfund.

Only afterwards did it occur to me that she could be a spy for the Eritrean government, that they could have found out which church had organised the demonstration and that this was the church that I attended.

I called an Eritrean friend and told her what had happened. She confirmed my fears. She told me the woman was based at the Eritrean embassy and was a member of the Eritrean political party. She was indeed a spy.

This incident marked a major turning point in my life. It helped shape the course I would follow in the years ahead. I now knew they were watching me, so I had little to lose by holding back.

Around that time, more Christians from an Eritrean church organised a demonstration outside the embassy. They were joined by representatives of other groups. One of the organisers was Selam Kidane, an outspoken psychologist in her late 20s, who would eventually become a co-founder of Release Eritrea.

I'd been following Selam's postings on Eritrean opposition websites and met her at the church. Her husband was an elder. Soon after, I was invited to join a special task force to campaign for freedom of worship in Eritrea.

Selam Kidane and I were called to meet the church elders. They said, 'We want you to be a voice for the persecuted church in Eritrea.'

I offered a note of caution: 'You know this will expose you to the attention of the Eritrean government and could cause division within the church?' I knew there were several church members still loyal to the Eritrean government who would continue to support them, no matter what. But the church elders believed they could win them round. So we accepted their commission to represent all the Eritrean churches across Europe.

All Saints Church and its leader Rev Marty Sunders played a key role in helping us establish Release Eritrea. The church had been paying me £2,500 a year for four years. It was intended as support for my family in London, as I was still studying and had no income, but I used the money to help prisoners of faith in the days before we began to get help from donors. That donation of £10,000 became seed money to establish Release Eritrea. And in 2009, when Release Eritrea registered with Charity Commission, we gave our office address as All Saints Church.

21

BACKLASH

One of the tasks for Release Eritrea was to write letters to the Eritrean embassy in London. We sent some but received no reply. Then Selam, my colleague, suggested writing an open letter to the Eritrean president. Nobody challenged Isaias Afwerki, who had spearheaded Eritrea's drive for independence from Ethiopia in 1991. To question his policies was to cross a fat red line that could prove fatal.

We posted an open letter to the president on the internet, and perhaps because of that we received a lot of criticism from church members in London. But we continued to call on the government of Eritrea to release its prisoners of faith and re-open the churches for worship. The website grew in popularity among the Eritrean diaspora.

Then the Eritrean embassy hit back. They told the church in no uncertain terms to put a stop to our campaign. One of the elders said we had become too militant and too hard-line on the Eritrean government. Some even suggested we were working for the CIA. Clearly the embassy had got to them. But I was defiant. I said, 'I will not stop until our brothers and sisters are released from prison.'

Selam and I decided to carry on independently. I'd been preaching regularly in the Betel Eritrean church in London. Now the pastor called me and told me that had to end. He said there was a problem in the church and I would no longer be invited to speak there.

I never want to cause friction in any church and I was well aware how the Eritrean government operated. I was sure the diaspora church was not yet ready to withstand well-organised attacks from the embassy in London. So I decided to pursue my advocacy work outside of any particular congregation.

By now, Selam and I were active on social media and in reaching out to news outlets. I'd been interviewed by the BBC and newspapers on the situation in Eritrea. Selam and I were determined to continue, and so in 2004 we created a new website: Release Eritrea. This was our introduction to many like-minded organisations.

During that time the Eritrean government continued to send Christians to prisons in all parts of the country. Christians were detained at wedding venues, arrested in house churches, hauled from offices, and even pulled from the streets. They were sent to prisons, labour camps and underground dungeons. Some were lowered into dugouts in the ground, hot, humid holes some four metres deep, with a roof and small opening at the top. They were incarcerated there with three or four other prisoners. It was like living in a sewer pipe. They would struggle to breathe and suffer infections.

We began getting reports from Eritrea about torture and parents being taken from their children leaving no-one to care for them. Release Eritrea suddenly became one of the most sought after and trusted providers of news about the developing situation. The arrests seemed so many – it was difficult to follow the news and record them all, but we put updates on our fledgling website as fast as we could. Between 2003 and 2004 hundreds of Christians were arrested.

By 2004 I'd finished my research and graduated with my MPhil. By now I was involved in separate work with a mission organisation in Llanelli, South Wales. My vision was to raise missionaries from the Eritrean diaspora and send them to the mission field, mainly in Arab countries. I went to Wales with my family and three other Eritreans and remained there for more than a year. But then we hit two serious problems.

We were funding this ourselves. Alem had to leave her job to relocate to Wales, and without her income our savings ran out. More to the point, so did my student visa. And having started work with Release Eritrea it would have been fatal to be sent back to my country.

All the senior pastors had been arrested and all my friends were in prison. If I were forced to return to Eritrea I would most definitely disappear and Alem would be left to live like a widow along with our daughter. Eventually, the Home Office granted me asylum. It was a relief to be allowed to remain, but my heart was still firmly in Eritrea.

Meanwhile, the arrests continued unabated. The second group to be taken were pastors from the Full Gospel Church. The Rev Haile Naizgi had worked with my wife at the Eritrean branch of World Vision International. He was a serious man of God. Dr Kiflu Gebremeskel was a university mathematics lecturer: smart, intelligent and a man of real integrity, well respected by Christians and non-Christians alike.

Dr Kiflu had given himself to full-time Christian ministry and had opened a Full Gospel Church in a southern district of Asmara. We had a similar vision. We prayed for Eritrea every Sunday evening at my home and discussed the possibility of working closer at some point.

The last time we spoke was over the phone while he was on a short visit to Germany. I was concerned for him. I could see what was coming. Perhaps it was easier for me to take stock of the situation in Eritrea from outside the country. I warned Dr Kiflu not to return. But although his church building had been shut down, the church had continued to meet in homes. It was doing well, so he intended to go back.

Dr Kiflu's approach had been to pray for the government rather than campaign against them. And he criticised me for taking part in demonstrations.

I had to disagree with my friend. I believe there is a time for challenging governments because it is sometimes necessary to address the human will. There are times when we must go beyond prayer, when we must challenge directly. Those who pray and those who act need to work together. But I truly respected Dr Kiflu as a man of God. He had written a book on morality and governance and sent it to the President. It was intended to be helpful and constructive but could well be one of the reasons he got into trouble.

Soon after we spoke, I heard he'd been taken by security forces in an early morning raid on his home. That was in 2004 – and he has never been released. His wife and children have never been allowed to visit him.

In the same month the government's security forces arrested two people from the Rhema Church, Pastor Tesfazion Hagos and a co-worker, Million Gebreselassie. Million had worked at Massawa Hospital as an anaesthetist. Pastor Hagos was released from prison after six years, largely for health reasons. He moved to Australia to join his wife and two children.

Later in 2004 the Eritrean authorities arrested three clergy from the Orthodox Church. One of them, Dr Fitsum Gebrengus, had been part of the Christian medical fellowship in Ethiopia in the 1990s. He was a gentle man, pale-skinned, bespectacled and serious about his work. At the time of his arrest, he was perhaps the only psychiatrist in the country. He was a committed doctor, who'd been working hard to improve mental health services in Eritrea. He was also a committed Christian, a good teacher and highly influential among the younger members of the Orthodox Church. He ran a highly successful youth group that was attracting thousands of young people.

The government was suspicious of any emerging movement, youth movements especially, so they arrested Dr Fitsum, even though no laws had been broken. Then they asked the Patriarch of the Orthodox Church to excommunicate Dr Fitsum along with his fellow ministers and the entire youth group for breaking Church law. The government demanded that the Patriarch excommunicate 3,000 members of the church. They set about arresting ministers.

Patriarch Abune Antonios, who'd spoken out against the persecution of Christians, protested. He refused to back down. He ruled that no church laws had been broken. Despite that, the government shut down the youth movement and called on Patriarch Antonios to resign.

When he refused, the government put him under house arrest and pressured the Eastern Orthodox Synod to replace him. This cynical act compromised the Orthodox church and fatally undermined its credibility.

Patriarch Antonios, who was 80 at the time, was put under house arrest in Asmara and held incommunicado. He was forbidden from attending church services and denied all visitors, including clergy and relatives.

According to reports, Patriarch Antonios was given the usual opportunity to confess his 'crimes' and purchase his freedom. But he refused to sign. And he refused to compromise his integrity and the integrity of his faith right up to his death 16 years later. He's been described as the longest-serving prisoner of conscience in the Horn of Africa.

This attack on the Orthodox Church and its Patriarch was an attack on every Christian in Eritrea.

Wherever there is an established church, it becomes the target of governments who want to manipulate the church for their own purposes. In my view, wherever there is a state church, the gospel will be compromised. How can a church which is part of the ruling system speak truth to power and challenge the government? The church must stand against all injustice and be ready to sacrifice its ministers for the sake of justice.

What is happening today in Eritrea and Russia has been happening in Ethiopia for centuries. Governments seek to use the church as an instrument of control. The church, in order to maintain its position in society, will persecute other Christians, even from within their own community.

So what of Dr Fitsum? This man who loved God, who loved his country and loved his congregation; and whose thriving youth ministry sparked off this backlash against the Orthodox church. Police seized Dr Fitsum as he was about to speak at a conference and imprisoned him indefinitely in Wenjel Mirmera, the maximum security Central Criminal Investigation interrogation centre. When his wife and father died, they refused to let him attend their funerals.

22

HELEN BERHANE

2004 was also the year that Christian gospel singer Helen Berhane was arrested. Helen was exposed to many hardships, including torture and all forms of physical and emotional abuse. But what captured the world's attention was that she, and others, were being locked away in steel boxes in Asmara, where they baked by day and froze by night. The authorities were keeping their Christian prisoners in shipping containers.

I had one of these containers in Eritrea for use as my office. And to try to regulate the temperature, I'd added insulation. But by day, it was still too hot, and by evening it was too cold. In the heat of summer it was an oven. And in the cold of winter it was a freezer. And my shipping container had a wide window and a wide open door. Unlike Helen's.

Our Release Eritrea team found a music album Helen had recorded and used the cover picture for our press release. Her story immediately struck a chord. She was one of the first Christian prisoners we'd heard of being tortured under this new regime, and one of the first to be kept in a shipping container – the first of an estimated 2,000 held that way over the years.

Amnesty International ran adverts with her picture in newspapers and her story was covered in many media outlets, including *The Guardian* newspaper in the UK.

In her book, *Song of the Nightingale,* Helen describes a freezing winter's night in that shipping container:

'A single candle flickers, it's flame barely illuminating the darkness. They never burn for more than two hours after the container door is locked: there is not enough oxygen to keep the flame alive. It will go out soon.

'Condensation drips from the roof and slides down my cheek, and when it moistens my lips I taste rust. The air is thick with a dirty metallic tang, the ever-present stench of the bucket in the corner, and the smell of close-pressed, unwashed bodies. I cannot believe that this is my life: these four metal walls, all of us corralled like cattle, the pain, the hunger, the fear. All because of my belief in a God who is risen, who charges me to share my faith with those who do not yet know Him, a God whom I am forbidden to worship.'

It seemed Helen was always in the news. I knew her parents. Her father and mother were both nurses. Helen's mother had worked on the ward with me when I was a doctor and I had given medical treatment to Helen when she was a teenager.

Later we heard that Helen had been confined to a wheelchair for a time. Eventually, she was released from hospital and allowed to go home. I was greatly relieved.

Due to tight security, I was unable to contact Helen while she was in Eritrea but learned she'd managed to get to Sudan. That troubled me. I was able to contact Helen and warn her that Sudan was not safe: Eritrean security agents were operating freely inside Sudan and were known to have kidnapped opponents of the regime. They were bribing the police to report any suspicious activities.

During Helen's 11-month stay in the country she moved house on four occasions. But even then, she wasn't safe. We campaigned for the British government to grant her asylum, but they refused. It was very sad. In 2007 she managed to secure asylum in Denmark.

Helen Berhane tells her story in *Song of the Nightingale*. In it she writes: 'I think back to a question I've been asked many times over my months in prison: "Is your faith worth this, Helen?" As the guards continue on their rounds, I whisper the answer: "Yes."'

And within those four steel walls, baking and freezing with crowded and unsanitary conditions, this gospel singer wrote a song, a song of love to the God who sustained her:

I love you, that's why I draw myself closer to you
I know that it's worth following you.
I am not only ready for prison, but I trust you until death.
Even in a closed space or in a pit I will not surrender to evil spirits,
Not even if I am bound or I am chained and I am suffering from cold,
I will sing and I am not going to tire of singing, nor give up.
My heart is burning with your love,
And my heart declares I will never stop respecting you or lifting you up.
I will sing again and again,
I will sing a melody for you,
My soul is pleased to sing for you.

In March 2005 we heard that another pastor in the Full Gospel Church, Kidane Weldu, had been arrested. I'd known Kidane since I was a child. He'd been raised in the same neighbourhood in Asmara and was a close friend of my older brother. Kidane had been a secondary school biology teacher before he gave his life to full-time gospel ministry. He never had the opportunity to see his family and has never been released.

We were kept busy at Release Eritrea, trying to post all the persecution news as it reached us. It wasn't easy and we had to be careful over what we said and how – we didn't want to make the situation worse for prisoners or to compromise their families. Yet we felt that we had to let the world know what was happening. We believed passionately that these prisoners were part of the body of Christ and therefore their suffering was shared by the worldwide church. My conviction was that they needed prayer and that we needed to advocate for their release.

Sadly, that mandate to speak up for suffering brothers and sisters in Eritrea wasn't observed by some sections of the Eritrean diaspora church. In December 2005, I was called by another pastor who told me I would no longer be welcome to preach at his church. I knew they were under pressure from the Eritrean embassy and that there were probably some members of the church who would always support the government there. It was tough to lose the fellowship and support of part of the Eritrean community. But I was not prepared to compromise on what, I believed, I was being called to do.

As I was meditating on the word of God the story of Esther in the Old Testament came to mind. Esther was inside the king's palace when a new decree was passed that would have led to the killing of all the Jews in that land. Esther made up her mind to act, even if it would cost her life. I believed God had brought me to the UK because he wanted me to be a voice for his suffering people.

Release Eritrea continued to be heavily involved with Christian refugees. Some Eritreans, who'd embarked on the hazardous journey to freedom in Israel, were kidnapped and held for ransom. Many who'd made it across the Sinai region were now living in Israel illegally, without support from the state. Many of these women had been raped. Because of that, they faced rejection from their husbands. Many more were being harassed and bullied. There were 10,000 Eritrean women refugees in the southern part of Tel Aviv alone. Where do you even begin with that?

An Eritrean refugee suggested starting a nursery, so women could leave their children and find work. That grew into a women's club, where women could come together, share their stories and get support. And from there it grew into schools to teach languages and computing, run by volunteers.

My colleague Selam Kidane suggested opening a safe house in Israel for women and built a women's refuge. It offered help to those who'd been abused by the people smugglers or their own partners and gave advice on seeking asylum and getting medical help. The centre quickly became overwhelmed by hundreds of needy women. It's still running and is now led by the women themselves. The project had a nursery for toddlers, a language school and we hired workers who could offer pastoral care to those who'd been abused.

Another big area of work was with refugees in Egypt. Thousands of Eritreans were fleeing to Sudan and then to Egypt, on route to Israel. These refugees faced persecution and abuse along the way. Some were sold into slavery. Those who resisted were often killed and their organs harvested for transplants. Release Eritrea rented three safe houses in different locations of Cairo. Many of the people we looked after had gunshot wounds. By 2012 we were supporting some 700 people and had hired four Christian workers to oversee their pastoral care.

On top of that, a large part of our work has been supporting refugees in Ethiopia, as many Eritreans had opted to flee over the border. There were four refugee camps in the Tigray region of Eritrea, each averaging between 10 to 15,000 people, a number which later grew to more than 20,000 in each camp. When I first visited these camps, the only thing these refugees had was a tent provided by UNHCR – The UN Refugee Agency.

The tents were hot and buzzing with flies and there was nowhere for anyone to sit. The family we visited tried to offer us coffee but couldn't find a mortar to grind the beans. Their three-year old child was sick with malaria. Others were, too. The toilet was filthy. There was no drainage. Mercifully, UNHCR were able to build houses and these camps eventually grew into towns.

We gave priority to ex-prisoners and women who'd been abused. Our primary role was to support the needy. Our work in the refugee camp encompassed pastoral care, Bible teaching and supporting the refugee churches that were forming. We helped the refugees start their own businesses.

It takes a lot of God's grace, as well as money and connections, to support Christian prisoners, their families and refugees. I was often overwhelmed with the stories of what was happening in the Eritrean church, of people in prison and the hardships they would face after they were released – *if* they were released.

There have been so many sad stories. In the summer of 2017, the government rounded up 200 Christians at the same time. Police had been trawling house-to-house to arrest them. A lady called Fikadu died three months after her arrest, after drinking contaminated water. That, and the effects of dehydration from the sweltering conditions, led to acute kidney failure. Her husband Afeworki was also arrested, along with their 17-year-old son. Both were released shortly after Fikadu's death. They were forbidden from attending her funeral.

That same summer another group of people was hauled off to prison, from the town of Adi Quala in the south of Eritrea. Some 35 children were suddenly left without parents to provide for them. The fortunate ones were looked after by other family members – but many were left on their own.

The prisoners were ordered to reconvert to their parents' religion. Since most were Evangelicals from an Orthodox background that meant returning to the Orthodox faith. Some were forced to go through a cleansing process by Orthodox priests.

In the Orthodox Church, this begins with a rebaptism to cleanse you of heresy. Every member is assigned a priest as a spiritual advisor. He will visit you regularly to check whether you are observing the Orthodox law and whether you are following a patron saint. He will require you to perform many rituals. If not, he will call on you to repent. Many evangelicals returned officially to the Orthodox Church, went through the process, but continued to meet secretly with other evangelicals. Those who refused to go back to the Orthodox religion are still in prison.

The arrest of all these Christians affected me personally. Many were elders of the church in Eritrea. Some were from a medical background, people I'd known for years. They were intelligent and smart – the cream of society. They were my friends and I would look back on the days when we went for coffee or a meal together.

Sometimes I would imagine myself with them in the prison because I knew the prison where they were, I'd been in that same cell, and I could picture them there. Sometimes I thought about the children growing up without their fathers and their wives, waiting, waiting, waiting; until they became widows even while their husbands were still alive.

These nightmares would recur two or three times a week. They were affecting my health. And in every dream, I would find myself among them. Sometimes I would be trying to escape. Somebody would report who I was, or I would find myself inside Eritrea, trying to leave, but unable to go through the airport, because my name was on a blacklist.

Today, I try to get less emotionally involved, to separate myself from my work. I have to remind myself to do that. Understanding some basic psychiatric principles and recognising symptoms helps because I have an insight into the human mind. But I am angry inside when I see Christians supporting the Eritrean government.

Amid all that pain and turmoil, which goes on to this day, the persecution has continued to grow, and the work of Release Eritrea along with it. We quickly realised we would need help.

23

RELEASE INTERNATIONAL

News about Release Eritrea's work began to spread in the Christian world. This led to the beginning of my relationship with a ministry that supports persecuted Christians in some 30 countries around the world.

UK-based Release International was inspired by the work of Pastor Richard Wurmbrand, who was tortured for his faith in Communist Romania. It was established in 1968 as Christian Mission to the Communist World but widened its remit and changed its name after the fall of the Berlin Wall.

I came across Release International at the New Wine event at Shepton Mallet. The organisation was passionate to help the suffering church and it was growing. Their emphasis was on prisoners, faith and mission rather than fundraising, which I appreciated. It was the beginning of an enduring relationship. Over the years, I have found Release International to be Christ-centred, prayerful and supportive.

In early 2005, I received a call from one of their staff, Colin Spence from Northern Ireland. Colin asked if I would be willing to meet him in London, so he could find out more about Release Eritrea.

We met in a café at Victoria train station. Colin said Release International wanted to support persecuted Christians in Eritrea but would need to know more. He asked me if I could take him to meet some of my countrymen and women who were suffering for their faith. It would be impossible to go to Eritrea, but there were refugees in Sudan and Ethiopia. The Sudanese government turned down Colin's visa request, so he, and three others from Release International, headed out to Ethiopia.

On the back of that pioneering trip Release International published stories about the persecution of Christians in Eritrea and the plight of Christian refugees in Ethiopia. Their magazine included testimonies from the Ethiopian refugee camp and launched a campaign encouraging UK Christians to pray and to act. Soon information about the persecution began to spread more widely through the organisation's news releases.

I was called on to speak at conferences organised by Release International and others, and began travelling to Europe, North America and Africa; highlighting the persecution of Christians in Eritrea. There were some angry exchanges in Ethiopia which taught me to keep a low profile about any future travels.

We began to hold prayer vigils outside the embassy in London, to pray and share Scripture and to show the Eritreans and the world that we were watching. A growing number of organisations were represented and eventually this prayer vigil became an annual event.

Throughout 2006 the persecution continued. My heart broke when I heard that a group of some 86 people had been arrested from one of my former churches in Eritrea. Many were children and young women.

They were taken to the notorious Me'etr Prison, in the remote north-west of Eritrea. It was hot and dusty, and anyone who tried to escape would be eaten by hyenas or die of thirst. To make matters worse, the prison was too remote for families to bring food, so many prisoners were starving.

One of the children they had taken was Rahel. She was just nine years old when she was imprisoned along with her parents. Other girls were only 15.

Mebrat, who was released after one year, is in her 20s at the time of writing and still living with her four children in an Ethiopian refugee camp. When I visited her, she told me that her husband is still behind bars. Mebrat is a committed Christian and an active member of a refugee church.

Another 16-year-old was arrested at that time. I will call her Shalom. She was ordered repeatedly to renounce her faith, but courageously chose to stay in prison rather than betray the Saviour who died on her behalf.

When the news of the arrests of these young children reached me, I cried and cried, and the nightmares returned. My days were taken up speaking and praying about these Christians in prison, and they filled my dreams at night. It was as though I was with them there, in person, sharing in their sufferings.

Christian friends reminded me that I had to find a way of emotionally separating myself from those who were suffering – but how? For me it was impossible. Every new report of someone being arrested pierced my heart. As the Apostle Paul reminds us, 'If one member (of the body of Christ) suffers, all suffer together.' (1 Corinthians 12:26).

The passage of scripture that sustained me is the verse that Release International takes as its foundation and frequently quotes: 'Continue to remember those in prison as if you were together with them in prison, and those who are ill-treated as if you yourselves were suffering.' (Hebrews 13:3). I was seeking to be obedient to this call in all that I was doing.

In 2007 hundreds more Christians were arrested. The most prominent were two pastors. Mussie Ezaz who, as a new believer, had been involved in a Bible study class in our house. The other was Okba, a passionate Christian who was tall, slim and always smiling. We knew him as a man of love, who was willing to give his life for others.

Okba had been raised in an orphanage and became a teacher there and then a pastor. Finally, he became the director.

The church was his life. The first time he was arrested, he was with a group of young people gathered to pray in a container we used as an outbuilding at church. Security services got wind of the prayer meeting and raided it. Okba tried to negotiate with these intruders. He said, 'This is my responsibility – take me, but not the children.' But they took them all, including the young children.

They arrested Okba twice more. The second time was for conducting a Christian wedding. They took Okba, along with the bride and groom, bridesmaids and all the wedding guests to a military camp. In 2007 they picked him up again for assisting a pastor who'd escaped from prison. They finally released Okba due to ill-health in 2018, after 11 years.

Over the years, Colin Spence, who'd connected me to the ministry of Release International, became a close partner in the ministry to the persecuted. Colin was good-humoured and fun-loving, but deeply serious about the work of God. He was a humble man who gave his all to the ministry. He befriended each refugee personally, would pray with them and knew them by name. He was a man who liked people and people liked him.

We were travelling together in Ethiopia, in Shire, a town known for its juice houses which sell mango, guava, avocado, papaya and other delicious fruit drinks. As we were leaving, Colin suddenly froze, with a look of dread on his face. He had lost his camera. The camera contained all the pictures he'd taken to tell the story of the Eritrean refugees.

We went back and searched the juicers, to no avail, then a restaurant we'd visited, and then our hotel. Colin was far more concerned about the pictures than the camera itself. But later that evening he opened his suitcase to find it sitting there, neatly packed where he'd left it and ready for our return trip home. We laughed and laughed, out of sheer relief.

The living standard for Christian refugees in the camps of Ethiopia has improved much over the years thanks to the ministry and on-going financial support of Release International. Release funded a credit scheme for refugees. One Christian helped by this programme was Abeba, who later moved to Addis Ababa in Ethiopia with her four daughters. Abeba was deported to Eritrea during the war of 1998. Her husband was arrested there for his Christian faith and sent to prison. He suffered from diabetes but was prevented by prison officers from taking his medicine and died soon afterwards.

Abeba fled to Sudan and ended up in the refugee camp in Ethiopia, which was where Colin Spence met her. He was so moved by her story that he arranged for funding to enable Abeba to open a bakery in Addis Ababa. That bakery did so well that by the time we visited in 2014 Abeba had been able to send her children to a private school.

With Release International's support other refugees were able to open coffee shops, photo shops, hairdressers, grocery stores and more. During one early morning visit to refugees, we were waiting for the camp to open and went into a roadside café for cold drinks. The owner immediately recognised us. He'd been able to set up that café through the support of Release International and was active in Christian work in the camp.

Colin and I travelled together to Paris to visit an ex-prisoner, Aster, whose twin-sister, Azieb, had been tortured to death in Eritrea. Aster was beaten alongside her sister but was already unconscious by the time Azieb died. She ended up in hospital and only learned about her sister's death weeks later.

Initially, Aster refused to talk about what had happened. It hurt too much. But eventually she agreed and told us her story for more than an hour.

The church had hired Azieb as an evangelist, trained her and assigned her to a remote church. When they arrested Azieb she was with her sister. They were taking part in a celebration for a Christian couple who wanted to renew their wedding vows. Sixty people had come along to join in and witness the occasion. But these large numbers drew the attention of the security police.

They broke up the event and ordered all the Christians to renounce their faith. Many of the men did. But a group of women refused, including Aster and Azieb. Some of them were as young as 15. And they ended up in a shipping container at Mai Serewa Prison.

Aster and Azieb were among a group of girls who'd been beaten repeatedly, exposed to the midday sun and were forbidden from taking a bath. In July 2008, the guards took them into the wilderness outside the camp to beat them, and it was there they killed Azieb.

It was difficult for us to control our emotions as Aster calmly told her story in a very composed way, quoting from Scripture and reflecting biblically on her experience. She reminded us of how Mary had watched as the guards had beaten her son Jesus. She said, 'I'm not better than Mary.' Aster was full of the word of God. Her sister had been the same. When you looked at her, you could see the grace of God. It was both moving and inspiring.

The last time I travelled with Colin Spence we visited Shire again to run training sessions with a group of Christians. The conference was followed by a meal. That night I came down with food poisoning. Colin and other members of the team were also sick. But for Colin the after effects dragged on for more than three weeks, and it seemed he was never really well after that.

A few months later I heard Colin had been diagnosed with cancer of the oesophagus. I knew what that meant – and it broke my heart. Colin continued to deteriorate physically until he went to be with the Lord a year later. But during that difficult time he remained full of faith and spiritually strong. It was a great privilege to attend his memorial service in Belfast.

Colin will always be remembered by the Eritrean Christians whom he befriended during his work with Release International.

The church in Eritrea had prayed for him, especially when he was ill.

Colin and I had dreamed about visiting Eritrea when things changed for the better. We'd prayed for that to happen. Sadly it was not to be. When a number of prisoners were released, I wished Colin had been alive to hear the news. Some were Christians he'd supported for years. But although I would have loved to have been able to meet and celebrate in this world, I'm comforted to know that we shall all meet once again before the throne of God.

24

DECISION TIME

For many years, I'd been following twin tracks in exploring my calling. Was it to be medicine or ministry? And which would better serve my persecuted brothers and sisters in Eritrea?

In London, I'd passed my Professional and Linguistic Assessments Board Test. This makes sure doctors who graduate abroad have the necessary skills and knowledge to practise in the UK. At the same time, I was looking into the possibility of ordination. And both came together at once. I was accepted to work as a doctor and to be trained as a minister of the Church of England.

I was caught in a dilemma. I wanted to support my family. Alem was working in a nursing home to make ends meet. If I took work as a doctor, I knew I would be better paid. But I also knew I would be kept incredibly busy for the first three or four years. Gradually the Lord's will became clear.

I chose ministry over medicine. And I don't regret it. I could have been a consultant, and I could have supported some patients, but there are many doing that. But this particular ministry to Eritrean prisoners – very few are doing this.

And today, when I hear testimonies from ex-prisoners, their families and refugees, I always thank God for helping me choose the right path. I can look back and be satisfied.

So having made my choice, I studied part-time for ordination with the South East Institute for Theological Education at

Southwark Cathedral. I was ordained in 2008. I called myself an Evangelical Anglican and did my training at St. Mary's church in Archway, Islington. Three and a half years later, I completed my curacy and started looking for a position as a vicar. And that's when things began to get difficult.

Every time I applied, I was told I was a good candidate but not right for that particular job. Some put it down to my accent. But my accent never seemed to be a problem with the people I served in Kings Cross when I first came to London. I'd been preaching on Sundays, taking part in the outreach, and connected well with everyone around. If the problem was my accent, then it was a problem for those in authority rather than the congregation. I was struggling to know why I was not accepted.

At one church I applied to, the incumbent carried out a pre-application interview. He asked, 'How do you feel about being black and serving in a church?' How do you answer that?

At Kings Cross we had all sorts, some Polish, some Greek – people from everywhere in the world. Many were having to be looked after by the state. There were alcoholics and drug addicts and when they were in trouble they came to me. They stayed with me and my family. They respected me. They didn't care about my accent or my colour. It was a friendly international church.

He asked me another question: 'How would you feel if somebody in the church was racist towards you?' I said it would depend who that person was. Some are racist out of ignorance, and I can tolerate that. But if that person was the minister, I would find that difficult.

Eventually, I was offered a house for duty, a vicarage without a salary. This was at All Saints and Holy Trinity church in Hackney. The post was for 18 months. After that I was asked to leave. I knew God would provide. It would need to be part-time work so I could continue supporting Release Eritrea. Eritrea is a part of me that will never die. Because the faithful believers I have met will never leave me. Believers such as Twen Theodros.

25

TWEN THEODROS

What would you do if you'd been thrown in prison just for being a Christian? If you were beaten, tortured, and knew of others who'd been killed, simply for refusing to sign a piece of paper that would put an end to all that suffering and set them free?

Would you sign?

Many Christians did just that; they gave their apologies to the state, they promised to forsake their religion, and they were released and able to go on with their lives.

What's the right thing to do? It is often not just a matter of our own lives or comfort, but the lives and security of those we love, who depend on us. It's about their future, too.

So what would you do?

I was given the ultimatum at medical college to sign a commitment not to preach the gospel or to leave. As I have said, I chose to leave. But what of those forced to endure much worse – both pain and mental torment, year in and year out?

I have learned not to criticise those who sign. There is grace enough for those who sign and for those who refuse. I will never belittle others for the difficult choices they are forced to make. Every choice has its consequences and each person must count the cost.

One prisoner in particular had to make that decision not once, but twice.

News reached me via an evangelist, who'd decided to sign and was set free, that there was one prisoner in particular who was bullying and persuading the others to refuse to sign. The story reached me that she'd made them swear never to sign this declaration. The Christian prisoners who had signed said this particular prisoner was giving all the others a bad name. Her name was Twen. And there was another side to her story.

Twen was arrested in February 2004 and spent one month in Mai Serwa prison. Her father came to her with a prison officer and the paper to sign. Twen later told Release International: 'My father begged me, saying he would allow me to read my Bible and have gospel songs, as long as I agreed to what the prison authorities asked in order to get released.'

Twen asked the prison official what it was she was saying yes to. He told her she was simply not to attend large meetings or to preach. Twen could still meet with other Christians, he said, but not in large conferences or gatherings; and she could share her faith with small groups but not to huge crowds.

It sounded reasonable. Twen was persuaded, she signed and just like that she was set free. But although they had shown Twen the piece of paper, she hadn't actually read it.

Twen had just finished her military training. So she was given a letter to take back to her unit. An officer opened it and read it to her. 'He said I had committed a crime and had signed to say I would go back to my former religion.' That was news to Twen. It came as a shock.

'My heart was filled with sadness. I knelt at my bedside and cried and cried. I asked God for forgiveness.' Twen put the letter inside her Bible and promised God that from then on, she would follow His word.

They arrested Twen again at a New Year's night vigil and took her back to Mai Serwa prison. And from then, Twen did her best to encourage other prisoners to refuse to take the easy way out and sign.

They threw her in a shipping container near Asmara with Helen Berhane, until Helen was released, and there Twen remained for an extended period in solitary confinement. The guards warned her: 'We will make you [renounce your faith] by force. If you do not comply, you will die.'

Two scriptures sustained Twen: Matthew 10:32-33, 'Whoever acknowledges me before others, I will also acknowledge before my Father in heaven. But whoever disowns me before others, I will disown before my Father in heaven.'

And during the hardest of times, when they closed off the ventilation to the shipping container until she was unable to breathe, the word that came to her was 1 Peter 4:12-14, 'Dear friends, do not be surprised at the fiery ordeal that has come on you to test you, as though something strange were happening to you. But rejoice inasmuch as you participate in the sufferings of Christ, so that you may be overjoyed when his glory is revealed. If you are insulted because of the name of Christ, you are blessed, for the Spirit of glory and of God rests on you.'

She said: 'I felt the Holy Spirit in my heart. I started to rejoice and breathe. It was like Daniel's friends alive [in the fiery furnace.]'

And as she was being beaten, God gave Twen a vision, just as he had given me. She said: 'I saw a man, who looked like Jesus, holding a girl in his arms. The girl was happy and having fun, but when I looked at the man he was in deep distress, because he was protecting her from the beating. I thought the stick is not falling on me, but on Jesus, so I was able to endure the beating.'

Twen endured 16 years in prison, before finally being released as part of a so-called 'goodwill' amnesty for 200 prisoners of faith in 2021. She told Release International: 'The grace of God made everything possible. I feel so blessed to participate in Christ's sufferings. The day I decided to choose the Bible over that letter was what sustained me in prison. It never came to my mind again whether I should renounce my faith. I had already made that decision.'

A longer version of Twen's story is given in the appendix to this book.

Astonishingly, Twen was still a new Christian when she was arrested. And she was one of the youngest Christians in the prison.

The measure of her character is this: at one point, they made it easy for her to escape. They let her out of prison for medical treatment. She was allowed to stay with her parents for a month. And throughout that time they brought pastors to visit her, and each who came tried to persuade her to sign the release paper. Her parents said, 'Do you think you know more than your pastors? Your pastors are mature. Some have been preaching for more than 40 years.' Many thought it was foolishness that Twen didn't try to escape. When God is giving you the opportunity to escape, why would you go back?

But Twen saw things differently. By now prison had become her church. She was with the other prisoners and God had given her a ministry among them. How could she flee and abandon her flock?

Looking back, I'm convinced Twen made the right decision. Because although she sacrificed ten more years, she invested so much in that group. And she gained the respect of the prison officers, who had no doubt that Twen was a genuine Christian.

Through all this, I never heard Twen complain about those who abused her. She continued to praise God. She told me the story of a group of Christians who came to visit her in Addis Ababa after her release. And they told her, 'God will repay you for all the sacrifices you have made.' They said God would give her a good job and a good house, but she interrupted: 'Wait, I didn't do this to gain anything. I did it as part of my worship. I did it for the One who died for me, who suffered on my behalf. If I did anything at all, it is no big thing.'

Twen expected nothing in exchange. She had come to understand the theology of suffering, the theology of sacrificing yourself for the sake of the gospel. She never saw herself as a victim, and she carried her cross willingly. She made that choice. And I respect that. As a result she became an inspiration to many. Many Christians from Ethiopia and Eritrea have told me about Twen. And all have said how they were comforted and inspired by her ministry and how her spirit was infectious.

Those, like Twen, who refused to sign took a stand for freedom – even though it cost them their freedom to make that stand. They had the God-given right to worship and they proclaimed it. And even their tormentors respected them because they saw their faith was authentic. And some prisoners who entered jail without faith, left there as Christians, because of the living witness of these Christian prisoners.

I met a man in the refugee camp in Ethiopia who told me he'd been jailed for four years. In that time he met Christians who were praying and reading the scripture. They were honest about their faith. He spoke to them and he was convinced. So by the time they released him, he was a Christian. I met another recently in Berlin, who had entered prison as an unbeliever, and went onto become a Christian minister. And that is because they closely observed the life of the Christians they met in prison.

The fact of the matter is, that while we trust God to deliver us from our enemies, sometimes He delivers us to them. Because He also loves our enemies.

26

DELIVERED TO OUR ENEMIES

As Christians our hope is clear: that God will deliver us from our enemies. But scripture shows us there are times when He delivers us *to* our enemies and into their hands. Think of Joseph, Daniel, Jesus and Paul, to name a few. And if He has delivered us to our enemies, for their sake, then that may impact our decision to search for an easy way out.

When I was arrested, I asked the Lord, 'Why am I here? What is your purpose?' I believed it was to be a minister for the gospel. And that is why every day I was preaching. I could not be sure whether I would live or die in that prison, but I was prepared to die for my faith. I said, 'As long as I live, I will be a true witness for the gospel of Christ.' So, every day, I took every opportunity to speak about Jesus.

One day, I was transferred to another wing for three days where I met a pastor who was arrested for his faith. He was praying and fasting for his own release and he wondered whether God had said anything to me about that. He was hoping for a word of confirmation. But I said as far as I was concerned, God wanted me to stay in this prison and to be His witness. The pastor was shocked. It was not the answer he expected.

At the time, he was being bullied by the Communists. Everybody was making fun of him, so when I could, I took the pressure off him and stood firm. Later, he said: 'Do you remember, when I arrived, you protected me?'

I wasn't scared of anyone. Not of the Communists, the prisoners of war, the Eritrean fighters or the other criminals. I was confident that God had put me there. God's word says, 'If God is for us, who can be against us?' (Romans 8:31). I knew God was on my side.

I was the happiest person in that prison. I was singing all day. I showed a different side of Christianity to the prisoners. I would challenge them, but I would also show them care and love. I knew I had committed no crime; I was there because that was God's plan for me.

In this cell were many who needed to hear the gospel, and many who needed to be comforted. All the prisoners lived in fear, but every day I would share from the book of Psalms. I would sing the Psalms and pray for the prisoners.

The Bible is a real comfort, because in a place like that there was no good news or word of hope. The Bible was the only thing that offered these prisoners any encouragement. So every day and every evening, they let me preach to the entire room. I would clap my hands and everyone would be quiet. Even the prisoners of war would stop talking and listen quietly. And shortly before he left the prison, one of those who just sat and looked away came over to me and said, 'The Bible is the greatest comforter.'

I shared from Psalm 23: 'Even though I walk through the valley of the shadow of death, I will fear no evil, for you are with me.' The men would look at me with wide eyes and after I finished they would come around. Everybody listened silently, even those who pretended not to.

Some would ask questions and ask for prayer. Some would ask me, 'Every day, we see you preaching and reading the scripture, but you have not been released. Where is your God?' And I would explain to them that I was not following God in order to get released. I was here for God's purpose to be fulfilled in my life. I told them, 'God has put me here for you.'

Some of those I shared with would lose their lives. Prison was a great opportunity for ministry, and I believe God delivered me to that place for that purpose.

In everything, we are in God's hand. At all times we are still God's children. Each of us has been purchased by the precious blood of Jesus. I knew the God who loves me would not let me suffer unless He had a purpose. So my main thought was, 'I don't belong to myself. I belong to Jesus, because I have been purchased by Him.'

I was encouraged when I began to see people getting converted. Many came for prayer for assurance and I was always saying, 'Don't be afraid, God is here.' The authorities were trying to rob us of our confidence and replace it with fear, but the gospel itself was building confidence and hope in the people. The last word belonged not to prison officers, but to God. And God had delivered me to my enemies to bring eternal hope to those they held captive. So, it was not for me to search for a way out.

When Jesus Christ gathered his disciples he told them, take up your cross, deny yourself and follow me. That's Christianity. When we decide to follow Jesus, we know what it means: it means to carry His cross and that we are to share in the suffering of Christ. So, if we are double minded, we suffer.

And I have seen prisoners who have made that choice to sign away their faith to find release and relief and who then live to regret it.

This is a cost we must consider and count in advance. Forgive me for putting you back in that uncomfortable place of dilemma: should you sign, or should you refuse to sign?

Let me help you to weigh that decision and count the cost by examining some of the justifications I have heard and their consequences.

While signing the government's piece of paper may have got them out of prison, the Christians who signed often felt guilty and ashamed. When they got out, they didn't want to see us. They avoided us to avoid having to face their own feelings. They no longer wanted to talk to us, even though we supported them for years while they were in prison. Most just wanted to put the whole thing behind them and stay out of trouble with the government. Some tried to pretend it never happened.

I have seen their depression, their sense of accusation and how they try to hide it. I have seen them haunted by what they have done.

The prisoners who decide to sign fall into two groups. One group say they signed because of their theology; they believe that suffering can never be the will of God, and that it is right for us to escape suffering wherever possible.

Some in this group have swallowed the notion that becoming a Christian will make you wealthy and healthy. So many in Africa are poor and they hope against hope that the way out of poverty is the Church. We see that reflected in the overemphasis on prosperity of so many African pastors. This is an unbalanced gospel that omits to remind us that along with enjoying the blessings of God we are to take up our cross.

Some of the pastors in prison tried to persuade the other Christians there to sign in order to get released. They wanted them to sign that paper so they would feel less guilty about signing it themselves.

Some went further. They tried to bully the other prisoners into signing by withholding their food. They accused them of causing more suffering for the church by being fanatical. They told them, 'The government thinks all of us are like you. But we're not. We support the government, and we obey the government. ou are bringing down the wrath of the government on the whole church.'

One Christian leader argued with another prisoner that God had told him to sign the paper and get released because He was about to bring judgment on the entire prison.

The prisoner who refused to sign was sceptical. She pointed out that if God were about to judge the entire prison for abusing the prisoners, then His judgment would inevitably fall on those prisoners who'd suffered abuse – which would make things even worse for them.

The church leader dug in his heels: 'If I were your pastor, I would force you to sign.'

She replied, 'If that's the case then I'm glad I do not have a pastor!'

It saddens me when church leaders are the first to sign. These are the shepherds. And some of these men who signed have gone on to become leaders of the church in the Eritrean diaspora and now call themselves apostles and prophets.

Another group believe they should stand up for their faith, and they really try, but are unable to tolerate the beating and the suffering, so finally they give up.

I have real sympathy for those who have tried because I believe that God understands them. He will never betray them and He will be faithful to them. We all fail. And our failure becomes part of our testimony. We're human beings. We break promises, we are afraid, and sometimes we lie, but we have a loving God who understands. Jesus has paid the price for human weakness. He will never give up on us, so we can continue in our faith. He will never give up on *us*.

For all our energy and all our efforts over all these years few prisoners are ever released without signing. Most are set free because they sign that piece of paper.

I try to encourage those who signed and now feel they have betrayed Jesus. I remind them that even Peter betrayed and denied Jesus in front of others when he said, 'I don't know him.' Fear overwhelmed Peter. He didn't know what he was saying, but he regretted it, he turned back, he repented. He cried and cried and cried. And he didn't try to justify himself. He needed mercy. He needed to be restored. And later he became willing to die for his faith and became one of the greatest disciples.

There are different levels of maturity and growth in the Church. Some Christians are not strong enough to tolerate the persecution. God understands and He still loves them. So that's why we try to support all the prisoners. Although we have special respect for those who endure and are faithful, we give financial support to those who have signed and to those who refused to sign alike. We don't discriminate.

And yet, I cannot help but cast my mind back to the Romanian pastor Richard Wurmbrand, who I heard speak those many years ago, the inspiration behind Release International; who refused to renounce his faith in order to escape imprisonment and torture. In his book *Tortured for Christ* he wrote:

'My mind was made up. I would not sign anything against my conscience. They were determined to break me. They tried every means. They tried to brainwash me. They tried to make me doubt my faith. They tried to make me hate. They used torture to make me confess to non-existent crimes.'

'I would rather die than betray my faith. I could not deny with my lips what I believed with my heart and my whole being.'

'I was beaten and kicked by the police and secret police, but even if they had killed me I would have died with the words "Jesus" and "love" on my lips.'

I had the privilege of hearing this exceptional man speak, in my own country; a man who, following in the footsteps of Jesus, counted the cost, paid the price, and became an inspiration for millions. I had read his book *Tortured for Christ* before I was converted. And when I decided to follow Jesus, Wurmbrand's suffering came to mind. But I had made up my mind, even unto death. That is why I was able to tell the Communist cadre, "For me to live is Christ – to die is gain."' (Philippians 1:21).

Ultimately the Church can only be built on authentic Christianity. The essence of the Church is Christ, and those who are willing to suffer for his sake and to die to this world.

We are encouraged and inspired by those who have embraced this and endured and have grown stronger and bolder in their faith.

They are our shining example.

27

SUFFERING SERVANTS

It's been my privilege to know many fine individuals who have suffered for their faith in Christ. There are a few more I would like to introduce to you.

Biniam Berhe is a gospel singer who was much-loved for his song-writing and musical gifts. He was known for introducing the traditional Eritrean circular dance into worship. His songs inspired many young people and it was these songs that led to his persecution.

Biniam was arrested in 2003 for his active Christian witness. He was put in solitary confinement and later imprisoned for about four months in an underground pit.

He described it as a hand-dug hole about four metres deep. The walls of this so-called cell were dirty and damp. There was a small opening in the roof, barely large enough to allow a little air to filter through. Biniam was in this cell with three others. They were allowed out twice a day to the toilet. They were the lucky ones. There were other prisoners who were never allowed to leave these holes in the ground. All the prisoners suffered from dysentery. There was no light in the cell and Biniam started to experience problems with his vision. He became so weak that he had to be taken to hospital.

In 2010, after seven years in captivity, Biniam and two other Christians made their escape. One evening they managed to dig a hole under the prison fence and fled. The guards spotted them and gave chase but lost them in the dark. They managed to hide in nearby cornfields, then split up to make their way to Sudan.

Biniam is now living in Canada and is active in a number of Christian fellowships. I asked him if he'd ever considered renouncing his faith, when he was first arrested, or at any time during his hardships in prison. His expression was resolute. 'Never, Berhane,' he said. 'Never would I have done that.'

Samuel and Merhawi were the two others who managed to escape with Biniam. Samuel – we called him Sami – was arrested in 2002, after the Eritrean authorities raided a worship service being held in a home. They took about 100 Christians that day. And they gave them all the choice: renounce their faith in Christ or go to prison. Many agreed and were released immediately. But Sami, Merhawi and the others who refused ended up in prison.

When they escaped, Sami got lost in the desert. Tired, hungry and thirsty, he lay down in a dried riverbed and was about to lose consciousness. A Muslim man on a camel was passing. He gave Sami water and sugar, put him on his camel and took him to a nearby village. He was a good Samaritan. After Sami recovered the locals gave him directions to Sudan.

Merhawi had also been arrested in 2002, as part of the big raid in Assab (see Chapter 20). He was a new Christian and yet when ordered to renounce his faith he refused. He was confused when he saw other Christians signing to get released. His mother came to visit him in prison and told him to sign the paper, but still he refused. His mother died while he was in prison.

Merhawi also got lost in the desert after they split up. When he finally got close to the border with Sudan he was confronted by an Eritrean soldier. The soldier asked for his identity card and realised he was not from that area. For some reason, Merhawi told the soldier he was a Christian and had been imprisoned for his faith for eight years. He added: 'Either take me to prison or show me the way to cross into Sudan.' The soldier laughed. He told Merhawi not only how to enter Sudan, but how to avoid any more Eritrean soldiers.

As he walked away the soldier called back, 'I am your Christian brother!' Merhawi is now also in Canada.

Timotewos is another Christian with an inspiring story. Tim was young and passionate about his faith. He had a real gift for sharing with others and was used by the Lord to bring many to Christ. He took dozens of new Christians to a village reservoir to baptise them. However, unknown to him, he was being monitored by the Eritrean security forces. They arrested him and sent him to Adi Abeto prison where he was badly tortured. This left him with a damaged back. Because of this he was in constant pain and unable to walk properly. While in prison he had to use crutches. Despite this handicap, he decided to escape.

Incredibly, he managed to walk out of this high security prison. He hid in the home of a Christian family for about a month, while the security forces were searching for him. Mercifully, they didn't find him. While in hiding Tim managed to put together a Christian worship album. Although he continues to have problems with his back, he remains full of life.

Yemane was arrested during national service in the Eritrean army. He'd been bold, active and persistent in sharing his faith among his fellow soldiers. Another soldier came to Christ after hearing Yemane preach. They executed that soldier and sent Yemane to prison. While there he continued to share the gospel and was regularly thrown into in solitary confinement as a punishment.

He later became severely dehydrated and passed out from heat exhaustion. He was so ill, they released him to die at home. But by the grace of God, Yemane recovered and went to Sudan for medical treatment, before ending up in an Ethiopian refugee camp. Yemane has since suffered a stroke and has a speech impediment. It can be difficult to understand him when he talks, but despite all he's been through, Yemane continues to share his faith and helps the poor at the camp where he lives.

Twen, Biniam, Sami and Merhawi, and many other unsung heroes remained strong in their faith, despite harassment and torture, suffering and sickness. They join those who remained faithful to the very end. 'They loved not their lives unto death.' (Revelation 12:11).

And yet... there have been so many deaths.

There are times when I blame myself, like a lazy shepherd who abandoned his sheep to the wild beasts. I survived because I got out of the country. Had I remained, I would have been number one on the hit-list. I felt like a bad general who sends his army into battle and his men to their deaths while he weathers the war in a place of safety.

One evangelist I sent out was assassinated while preaching. Another died under torture. These are people I recruited, commissioned and sent on their way. Others are still in prison. Some who were close friends have been behind bars for 19 years.

All this I must live with.

But I have come to accept that it was not I who sent them out, but the love of Christ. The initiative was Christ's and they were responding to His calling. They stood firm and they were faithful unto death. They received the grace to do so from God. This is not cheap grace. It cost them their lives.

Even so, this plays on my mind. When I hear about a death, I remember how they started, how each began their Christian journey.

When Azieb died, I started to blame myself. I remembered our first meeting in the container at church I'd used as an office. Azieb ended up in a container. And she was tortured to death for refusing to renounce her faith.

When I heard about her death, I struggled with my own faith. Azieb was one of the most loved and precious sisters.

She was so bold. She wouldn't compromise her faith for anything. She didn't care whether we paid her or not to do the work of an evangelist, she was so close to the gospel. That's why she was so badly tortured and ended up dying, because the guards considered her the leader of the group.

I questioned the Lord, and He said nothing at the time. But I was comforted when I met Azieb's sister Aster in Paris and heard all the details. Yes, Azieb had died at the hands of evil, but the Lord had a purpose. He wanted to show the church that nothing can stop the gospel, not even death.

When Stephen was martyred in the book of Acts, the people fled, and many probably wondered why. But because of what happened to Stephen, the gospel spread outside of Jerusalem. If it hadn't been for his death, the Christians would have stayed in the comfort of their city. But they – and the good news along with them – were scattered because of Stephen.

In Eritrea, the gospel has spread in an exponential way. Before the persecution, we were adding very few to the church, because Eritreans are a very conservative people. They are proud of their religion, whether Orthodox or Islam. So converting to another faith is unthinkable. Given that, it was hard to share the gospel. But when persecution came, hundreds and thousands of desperate people were thrown together in prison and came into close contact with Christians. Many more came out as Christians than those who went in.

One prisoner who did not convert to Christianity talked openly about her experience in prison on YouTube. She said the only consolation the prisoners received in that place was from those who had been arrested for their faith. The Christians, she said, had been a great comfort. And through them, her attitude towards Christianity changed.

Sometimes we must wait patiently to see the fruits of our labours. Our eyes must be on obedience, rather than reward.

28

CARRYING THE CROSS

Those who've been in prison and have suffered for their faith can be divided into those who cope and those who don't. Those who cope tend to be those who look on their experience as an opportunity, indeed, as part of their mission. Those whose prime concern is their personal release are the ones who continue to suffer, who see being in prison for ten or 12 years as a waste of time and a waste of life. And that has led some to suffer a nervous breakdown.

From my own experience and that of others, what I've learned is that to be persecuted for your faith in Christ is not a curse, but a God-given opportunity to go to places of suffering and share the gospel of Jesus.

When I was arrested all those years ago, I was a fairly new Christian, but I understood that I would not be there had it not been God's purpose for me to share the gospel. I was ready to die, but I was also ready to serve while I lived. And that led to harassment in prison from Communists pursuing their Marxist ideology and philosophy.

Over the years, the situation facing Christians in Eritrea has grown worse than when I was first arrested under the former Ethiopian regime. Today, prison itself might not even be a building, it could be a hand-dug hole and sometimes the open desert. For many it has been the barbaric incarceration in a shipping container – roasting by day and shivering by night.

There are some 350 prisons in Eritrea and close to 50,000 prisoners. Most are prisoners of conscience for their political views or their faith. Some are just ordinary businesspeople.

In this life Christians suffer in two ways: they 'carry the cross' or have a 'thorn in the flesh'. The thorn in the flesh might be sickness or national disaster, like a pandemic or an earthquake. At such time, Christians suffer along with others. But then there is persecution – and that is carrying the cross. Many Christians in Eritrea suffer both. They may suffer from a lack of food and medicine – shortages that impact the whole country. But at the same time, they have to carry their cross and they have to suffer for Christ.

Some Christians were very young when they were imprisoned for their faith. One girl was just 16 when she was arrested. She was jailed for 14 years. I think about people like that, growing up in prison. It's hard to see how these children would develop to understand the world. But so many Christian prisoners I've met are happy and are encouraged by what God has done for them. They have stories to tell, but they never focus on saying bad things about the government. Instead, they praise God for his provision. They want to tell you about the opportunities they've had to share their faith with those in prison with them.

At the same time there are those who have struggled, even after their release. One lady had been in prison for about five years, and later became suicidal. After her release, people said she'd wasted those years; she had nothing – no work, no husband, no children. Eventually she tried to take her own life. Thankfully, with the help of other Christians, she managed to escape the depression. She is now living in Ethiopia serving the Lord in a fruitful and very productive ministry.

Another prisoner had been jailed for 16 years. When he was released, he didn't want to talk about anything. He left Eritrea and our networks are still helping him. But when asked,

'What do you want to do now?' he said, 'Nothing.' It was as though his mind had been erased.

I think of another prisoner who became angry. He was released after 12 years and suffered a kind of post-traumatic stress disorder. His wife couldn't understand him.

The suffering doesn't end after someone has left prison. Yet we are not always alert to the after-effects of persecution. If you hold an animal in captivity for ten years and release it to the bush, it will not automatically behave like a bush animal; it may have grown more timid than others of its kind.

I have seen Christians like that, who struggle with life after a harsh spell in prison. And I ask myself, how can we help? How can we get them medical support? As long as they remain in Eritrea there are few medical facilities for them. The government has destroyed so much of the country.

And yet when it comes to persecution, I can still see the positive things. God is still in charge. He is still on his heavenly throne. He is still sovereign and at work. I believe we have more Christians in Eritrea now than when the persecution began. Christians have become bolder in sharing their faith and wiser in running an underground church.

At a refugee camp in Ethiopia, I met a Christian who'd been in prison for four years. His crime was failing to report that two people who visited him after his wedding were talking about leaving the country illegally. Every Eritrean is expected to act like a member of the secret police. If you hear anything said that could reflect badly on the regime you are supposed to report it and if they discover that you failed to do so you can be sent to prison for up to five years.

This man ended up in prison and while he was there he met Christians. They talked to him about Jesus. They shared with him from the Bible and he gave his life to Christ. After he was released, he escaped over the border with his wife, and that was how I met him.

Stories like these produce mixed feelings. They leave you sad and angry about the way people are arrested and treated – but also happy because you see a purpose for Christians being in prison for their faith. They are there to serve others and they are there to tell others about Jesus.

We are not called simply to preserve our own lives. Jesus said: 'If anyone would come after me, let him deny himself and take up his cross and follow me.' (Mark 8:34). To deny ourselves, follow Jesus and take up our cross may be mean suffering – but that's how God's work is being done.

To listen to some, Christianity is reduced to: 'If you follow Jesus you will prosper, you will be happy, and you will not suffer.' But what about those who *are* suffering? Is their faith inferior to yours?

Jesus called his disciples for this purpose: they were to serve him even when they suffered, in order to tell the world about the gospel. And prison is one of the places where that happens.

God sends disciples, preachers and evangelists everywhere. There should be no barriers. Prison is not a barrier and a Communist regime or a Muslim-majority country is not a barrier. That's how Jesus prepared his first disciples. He wanted them to go everywhere and that's what they did. They were strong in preaching the gospel. They preached to the Jews and they preached to the Gentiles. They preached in all sorts of places and in so doing they suffered. They were prepared to pay the price.

They understood that Christianity is not a club you join. It is the laying down of your life. It is self-sacrifice. You die to this world and are raised up with Christ.

The Apostle Paul wrote: 'We rejoice in hope of the glory of God. Not only that, but we rejoice in our sufferings, knowing that suffering produces endurance, and endurance produces character, and character produces hope, and hope does not put us to shame, because God's love has been poured into our hearts through the Holy Spirit who has been given to us.' (Romans 5:2-5).

Suffering is a fact of life. And it is a fact of the Christian life. We don't simply rejoice in glory or because we are prospering, healthy and safe. We are called to rejoice in our suffering, because through that suffering, we develop character; we develop this uniqueness: we start to look like Christ.

And so, we are hopeful. This hope is not in vain. This hope is not just in our minds. This hope is real. That is why Paul says hope does not put us to shame. Politicians offer many promises that can never be delivered. But what you get from God is real. God has flooded our hearts by his Holy Spirit.

29

SPEAKING TRUTH TO POWER

I have been engaged in this ministry since 2002. And although I live in the UK free from persecution, part of me is in Eritrea. So, I cannot rest. I feel the pain of Christians in Eritrea every day. The Apostle Paul was always in pain, sometimes because he suffered himself and sometimes because he was thinking and praying about the suffering church. There is only one body of Christ.

Whether it's the Church that's suffering in Eritrea, meeting secretly in homes or in prison, or in refugee camps in exile, these churches are the same. The way we meet, the way we study, the way we do church might differ, but we all worship the same Christ. We are all the one body of Christ.

And if one part suffers, the whole body suffers. Sadly, what I have seen over the years is how passive the Church can be when it comes to engaging in support for those Christians who are suffering.

I am now an associate minister, serving two local Anglican churches at Plumstead Common United Benefice. I'm also ministering once again to a church behind bars, as a chaplain at Thameside Prison. Sometimes I share about those in Eritrea, and the inmates pray for their brothers and sisters in prison there. In the UK or Eritrea, the prisoners know full well that we worship the same Jesus.

Of all the churches I have served in England it has been easier to share about persecution with the English church than the Eritrean diaspora. The English church is willing to engage and understand. A lot of church members support Christian mission. So, for a small church, they always contribute financially and there are some who are active in prayer.

I must confess I'm a little disappointed with the Eritrean church. I know some individuals do pray and offer their support, but much of the church appears to pretend that nothing is happening. And some try to politicise our concern. They say that to speak out about what Eritrea is doing to Christians is to disobey our government, and they quote from Romans chapter 13 to support that: 'Let everyone be subject to the governing authorities, for there is no authority except that which God has established. The authorities that exist have been established by God.' (Romans 13:1).

But it is a mistake to take these verses in isolation. We must draw on the full counsel of God. The German people misapplied those few verses to justify their silence about the rise of Nazi Germany. We have to consider the scriptures in the wider context.

My concern with the Eritrean church in the diaspora is not so much about the individuals as the leadership, which appears uninterested in supporting the persecuted church of their homeland.

We must speak the truth without compromise. The body of Christ is suffering. In the scriptures, all the prophets were persecuted because they challenged the authorities. In the Old Testament, they spoke against their kings. Some were thrown into prison and some were put to death. Many were executed. Even in the New Testament, John the Baptist was beheaded because he challenged King Herod. Paul challenged the authorities, knowing it would get him into trouble. But he continued to preach the gospel and declare the truth. He was almost certainly beheaded, too.

Scripture tells us we cannot worship two gods, that we must decide whom we will serve. In the Nuremberg trials after World War II, a judge questioned the leading Nazis: 'Why did you do this?'

They replied, 'We were following orders.' But they neither followed nor obeyed the higher orders, those orders we have received from God. So, to those who say we must obey our earthly leaders, I reply, 'Yes, but our first duty is to obey the higher authority.' We cannot be subject to unrighteous and ungodly laws. Our example is Daniel, who disobeyed King Nebuchadnezzar in order to remain obedient to the living God.

30

OBEY THE CALL

During the last 20 years I've been engaged in holistic ministry, working for social justice alongside the gospel. At the end of the day people need help and they also need to hear the good news of Jesus Christ. Ministry has meant caring for the whole person, to speak to the spirit and to care for the body also. In this, God has opened many doors for me through the ministry of Release Eritrea, such as working with refugees in Egypt, or starting a centre for women in Israel.

There are challenges as well as comforts when you see God's hand in all things. At the end of the day my heart fills with joy to be a servant of Jesus because I see him at work in other people's lives.

I have learned that not every disappointment is bad and a setback can be God's leading and guidance. Whenever I confront an obstacle I ask God, 'OK, why? What do you want to teach me – are you pointing to a change in direction?'

Since I began speaking out against persecution in Eritrea many have warned me how dangerous this is, because the Eritrean government has their trained assassins and geography is no protection. But when people remind me of this I say, 'When I decided to follow Jesus Christ, I gave my life to die.' And that means being willing to live for Him as well as die for Him. It means dying to my own plans and living for His.

My plan was to return to my country after my studies, but that would have meant returning to prison, and that was not how God was calling me to help my people. Accepting His will for my life was a major turning point. Accepting that I was called to ministry rather than medicine was another.

To begin with, many were challenging me: 'What do you expect to achieve? The Eritrean government will never listen, nobody can challenge them.'

And I told them, 'I'm just trying to do the right thing. I'm trying to live out my calling.' One asked me, 'How can we know whether God is guiding us or not?'

In the end, we have to follow our conscience. And when I do that, I feel satisfaction in my heart. I did not set out on this course for financial or worldly gain. I did it to do the right thing. What made me stand for the persecuted church was God's word, and I had to obey. The Bible verse that inspired me was Ephesians 2:10 'For we are his workmanship, created in Christ Jesus for good works, which God prepared beforehand, that we should walk in them.' I believe every person has been created to do good, and I believe it is my calling to do good in every circumstance.

When Daniel refused to eat forbidden food or to stop praying to God, many challenged him and asked, 'What are you trying to achieve? Are you taking on the king of Babylon, the greatest king of our time?'

But Daniel did the right thing and God heard his prayer. It was the same with Joseph in the Bible. He was the youngest and least significant of his brothers. He was thrown into a pit and sold into slavery. But it was Joseph who saved Israel from starvation and delivered the Israelites.

So sometimes, if we do the one small thing we feel God is asking of us – perhaps a prayer or a simple act of kindness – when we follow God's guidance, we can achieve the unimaginable.

When we began this ministry, we never imagined we would send millions of pounds to Eritrea – so much money that would be of so much service to so many.

Obedience has to be walked out one step at a time. And we are sowing seed with every step. For this reason, we must take care how we walk. We must never do anything contrary to the word of God. But if we agree with God and do what is right, if we walk carefully and work carefully, although we may not see the outcome, our walk and our work will be blessed and bear fruit. It might take years, but we will not remain without a harvest.

When we first started this ministry, we were ridiculed by both the government and the church. Everybody saw us as nobodies. We were allowed neither to preach nor to minister. We were like the seed that must fall into the ground and die. But God takes that seed and makes it grow.

The only thing we knew for sure, when we heard of Christians being arrested was that we had to be a voice for the voiceless, we had to speak up for them and be fearless. That's what the scripture says in Proverbs 31:8, "Speak up for those who cannot speak for themselves."

So that's what we set out to do. And it has grown from there.

God wanted us to speak up for those who could not speak for themselves, because they were in prison and had no voice. But we were here, we were free, and we could speak up for them. We were inspired by Hebrews 13:3, that we should put ourselves in their place, as though we were suffering alongside them. 'Continue to remember those in prison as if you were together with them in prison, and those who are mistreated as if you yourselves were suffering.'

Obedience to this calling has opened a door to the remarkable heroes of the faith in Eritrea, whose stories fill these pages; it has given them the opportunity to inspire a generation. And all this has emboldened me and emboldened others.

Today we see hundreds of thousands of Christians prepared to join us in crying out in prayer for their persecuted brothers and sisters in the body of Christ.

Each of us is a hero, as we listen to what God is saying and obey His call.

This, then, has been my story and theirs. I have tried to explain what I have come to understand about persecution, from my own experience and that of my friends who have suffered for their faith.

And having listened to our stories, it is over to you.

Having heard our hearts, my prayer is that you will hear the heart of God, and consider how, then, will you live, and what, then, will you do?

'For to me to live is Christ, and to die is gain. If I am to live in the flesh, that means fruitful labour for me.' – (Philippians 1:21-22)

APPENDIX: TWEN'S STORY

Following Jesus even unto death

by Tom Hardie
From Release International's Voice magazine
www.releaseinternational.org/magazines

Twen Tedros endured immense brutality during 16 years in Eritrean prisons – yet emerged victorious. Her inspirational story is a testimony to God's grace and your prayers.

Twen had been a Christian for only two of her 21 years when she was arrested and imprisoned. She was to spend the next 16 years locked away inside the Eritrean prison system, suffering intense persecution for her faith, yet knowing the grace of God sustaining her through every trial.

'I was raised in Asmara [the Eritrean capital] and brought up a Catholic but I began to question some of what I was told, and when I looked at my Christianity I saw I was lukewarm. After reading the Book of Revelation, where it warns about being lukewarm, the fear of God entered my heart. I thought God might spit me out!'

Despite pressure from her family, which included taking away her Bible and tapes of gospel songs, Twen began to meet with other committed evangelical Christians for worship. However, her freedom to express her new-found faith did not last long. She was spotted leaving a meeting and subsequently arrested.

In Eritrea there are only four permitted religions: Sunni Islam, Eritrean Orthodox, Roman Catholicism and the Lutheran Church.

'In February 2004 I was in prison for one month for my faith. My father came and begged me, saying he would allow me to read my Bible and to have gospel songs, as long as I said "yes" to what the prison authorities asked in order to get released.

'I was so happy when my father came, but I asked the prison official what I was saying "yes" to. He said it was simply not to attend any meetings or to preach.

'I replied that the Bible said not to abandon meetings. He said I could still meet but just not attend huge conferences or gatherings. I said, "What about preaching?" He said I could share with small groups but not huge crowds, so I agreed. I did not go into the details, but I signed and was released.

'At the time I had just finished military training, so they gave me a letter to take to my unit. When I handed over the letter to the officer, he said I had committed a crime and had signed saying I would go back to my former religion.

'I told him I had not said that, so he handed me the letter. [When I read it] my heart was filled with sadness and I went home and knelt at my bedside and cried. I asked God for forgiveness.'

Twen then put her Bible in front of her and pictured in her mind the paper she had signed, putting them side by side. 'I said to myself: decide. The Bible or the letter? Was I ready to forsake my family, my education, my job, all the things I love the most? And what about my life? I remembered that verse about forsaking everything for Christ. I made a decision there and then.

'For eight months after that I was filled with joy and freedom and felt no fear.'

However, Twen was to face arrest again following a prayer vigil on New Year's Eve 2004.

Twen was taken to a prison at Mai Serwa near Asmara where she would spend nearly three years locked away in a shipping container. Among her fellow detainees was Helen Berhane, the gospel singer. The two became close friends and when Helen was released Twen described it as the hardest time for her.

'I was on my own in the container. Many believers, mainly teenagers, came in and out of the prison, all renouncing their faith in order to get released. This even included pastors, so the prison officers put pressure on me, saying, 'We will make you [renounce your faith] by force. If you do not comply you will die.'

'I had only one verse in mind [Matthew 10:32-33] and I was resolved to obey it: "Whoever acknowledges me before others I will also acknowledge before my Father in heaven. But whoever disowns me before others, I will disown before my Father in heaven."'

During the daytime the prison guards would shut the door of the container and the window fully. 'I was not able to breathe. The guards waited outside for me to call them, but I prayed, 'Please God help me!'

'God gave me the word in 1 Peter 4:12-14, "Do not be surprised at the painful trial you are suffering, as though something strange was happening to you. But rejoice that you participate in the sufferings of Christ, so that you may be overjoyed when his glory is revealed. If you are insulted because of the name of Christ, you are blessed, for the Spirit of glory and of God rests on you."'

'When I received this verse, I felt the Holy Spirit in my heart. I started to rejoice and to breathe – I don't know how. It was like Daniel's friends still alive in the furnace. God wanted to show his glory in my life.'

Alone in the shipping container Twen says she learned the importance of Christian fellowship and says her suffering would not have felt so bad if she'd had other believers with her. However, when they realised she was determined not to renounce her faith, they sent her to another prison in Wia, on the Red Sea coast, one of the hottest places in Eritrea.

Twen was held in an underground cell but says, 'I had a heart full of joy because I was with other Christians.' In fact, such was her delight at once more being able to share fellowship that she described meeting these Christians as 'the day I was released!' Suddenly Psalm 133 took on a whole new meaning:

> *How good and pleasant it is*
>   *when God's people live together in unity!*
>
> *It is like precious oil poured on the head,*
>   *running down on the beard,*
> *running down on Aaron's beard,*
>   *down on the collar of his robe.*
> *It is as if the dew of Hermon*
>   *were falling on Mount Zion.*
> *For there the Lord bestows his blessing,*
>   *even life for evermore.*

Twen spent nearly two years in Wia where conditions were brutal. 'They tried to scare us with warnings that unless we renounced our faith we would suffer, but our position was to be faithful even to death.'

It was not long before their resolve would be put to the test. The guards started the beatings in the hottest season. One night they took Twen and others barefoot to an area with thorny ground. 'We had to run after one of the guards while another pushed us from behind.' Her feet became full of thorns.

'After a long time they made us lie down on the thorns and three men beat each woman. They were well trained in torture – they beat us in one place on our bodies again and again [making sure that] we would not pass out and get relief. They wanted maximum pain.

'After my beatings they made me sit down and said to me, "You're young, well educated, and you should get married and have children. We are giving you an opportunity to go because we love you and have pity for you".

'They were polite and tried to convince me. While in pain I answered: 'God gave me life; to give Him my life is a small thing.

'When they knew I would not give in, they reverted to cruelty; they hit me in the same place on my back. I could not tolerate the pain – it was beyond what I could endure, and I said to the Lord, "Don't test me beyond my ability to cope."

'And from then I saw the suffering as a great privilege and felt the Holy Spirit's presence. I received grace to endure the pain, and when I looked at the people who were beating me, I realised, I am suffering now, but this will take me to glory; they are laughing now, but their end is in loss; they are in a worse situation than me.

'I started to love them, and at that moment a verse from the scripture came to my heart and I prayed: "Forgive them, for they know not what they are doing". So I finished that night in victory!'

It was not just the beatings that prisoners were made to suffer but the effects of dehydration – they were given one just one cup of water and one piece of bread a day. Thankfully, Twen managed to survive.

Unsurprisingly, Twen questioned why all this was happening to her as she prayed for help. 'I was so scared. I said I cannot do this on my own as I am overwhelmed with fear.'

Then God gave her a vision: 'A man, who looked like Jesus, was holding a little girl in his arms. The girl was happy and having fun, but when I looked at the man he was in deep distress because he was protecting her from the beating. His mind was one hundred per cent focused on protecting the little girl. Then as they beat me, I thought the stick is not falling on me but on Jesus, so I was able to endure the beating.

'I knew I could not do it alone, but God enabled me. I had a wound on my thigh for many years afterwards. Jesus was always with me in the suffering, so even in that we are victorious.'

Because the guards believed that Twen was the leader of the group and that she was convincing others not to renounce her faith, they beat her even more harshly.

'They hit me everywhere on my body, and when I reached the place where I could not tolerate it any more I fainted. But they would wake me up. They were trying to get me semi-conscious so I would sign the document. When I had nothing to say the beating would continue and I would lose consciousness again.

'The third time this happened, I saw my soul separated from my body. I heard angelic songs and felt fresh air on my face. I experienced joy I cannot explain. When I woke up it was the hardest thing. I had been in a heavenly state and now I was surrounded by these men. I asked God: "Why did you bring me back? It's better to be with you." But it was not possible, and I started to give up hope.'

Twen had to be carried back to her cell. The prison governor told her she would die unless she went to hospital, but that she had to renounce her faith before she could go. Twen refused. She was taken back to the underground cell, along with another girl who had been beaten with her.

'I was in and out of consciousness. While we were lying there in the dark, I felt a sting on my foot. It was different to the usual bites of mice, and when the girl lit a match we saw it was a snake!' In fact, there were two snakes, and one was a large yellow cobra.

'The sister with me hit the snakes with a broom and managed to kill the smaller one, but the other was too big, so we prayed

David's prayer when he faced Goliath: "You come against me with sword and spear and javelin, but I come against you in the name of the Lord Almighty, the God of the armies of Israel.

'When we proclaimed this word our fear disappeared. One of the guards heard the noise and came to see what was happening. The large cobra next to me was about to strike. I was in so much pain that I could not move – but the guard just ran away and left us. "OK, but at least leave us your stick and flashlight!" pleaded my companion.

'As the snake was about to spit venom, we proclaimed David's word and then the girl hit it on the head. The cobra threw its whole body at us. I used the stick to fix it against the wall and we were able to kill it. God saved us. When the guards came back in the morning, they were surprised to see the dead snakes.

But Twen's whole body was already swelling. 'It was a miracle I survived; like Daniel not being eaten by the lions.'

Despite the swelling, the guards forced Twen to walk across hot sand, which burned her feet. 'When the guard pushed me to run the swelling in my foot burst. The pain was excruciating – the worst I'd ever felt. I cried like a child. No one could comfort me.'

As well as having to deal with their own physical pain, Twen had to watch as others suffered similar brutal treatment. On one occasion, twin sisters were beaten next to each other so they would have to listen to the screams of their sibling. After two hours, both lost consciousness. Twen held one of the sisters in her arms as she died.

'There's nothing good in prison,' says Twen. 'Everything is painful: the food, the water, the lack of clothes. In the first few years when I was sick, I was not allowed to see a doctor. Every day the guards use abusive words, they belittle you, mock you and try to break you. But in all of this, the grace of God was with me.

'What made the suffering easier was the fact that I was prepared. The day I decided to choose the Bible over the letter was what sustained me in prison. It never came to my mind again whether I should renounce my faith. I had already made that decision.'

Twen spent 16 years in prison, finally being released as part of a government 'goodwill' amnesty for 200 prisoners of faith.

When she reflects on her time in prison and all the suffering she has endured and witnessed, she has this message for Christians in the 'free' world:

'Your prayers saved me. This victory is a victory for all of us.'

'The grace of God made everything possible. I feel so blessed to participate in Christ's suffering. Even now, I do not have any grudge or hatred against those who put me in prison and tried to make my life miserable. I cannot think anything against them but love them.'

God never promised that we would not suffer in this world, 'But, says Twen, 'Christian prisoners will be thinking: "How can all this suffering be turned to good?" Pray that they can see an answer. I always pray that the same grace that sustained me will sustain them in their suffering; that they can rejoice. Suffering in this world is very brief and passes quickly, but God sees the eternal glory when he looks at us. He focuses on the eternal joy.'

Take my Life

by Michael Griffiths
OM Publishing
ISBN 1-85078-367
First published in 1967

> *Take myself, and I will be*
> *Ever, only, all for Thee.*

The aim of this book is to urge action. We have tried to make it plain that being a Christian means that we are, by definition, called to action.

We are not to be passive spectators of 'religion', content with a weekly appearance in 'church', but we are to devote all our energy, gifts, intellect and imagination to the passionate service of Christ.

We are to love God with all our heart, and soul, and mind, and strength.

It is not enough to carry our Bible with us to Church, where we may be instructed in the faith, but it must be translated into terms of daily living and enthusiastic obedience.'

Suggestions for prayer and meditation

Am I rejoicing in being joined to the living vine and am I bearing fruit for Him?

Am I busily engaged in Christian activity as a matter of duty or habit without a real sense of dependence upon the Holy Spirit?

Is my quiet time one of arid study and dry prayer or do I find the Lord is teaching me His will and this prompts me to a warm response in prayer?

Are we trusting in meetings, organisations, methods, committees – instead of trusting more directly in the power and guidance of the Holy Spirit?

Have I made a full committal of myself to the Lord Jesus and given him all my members, my faculties and gifts as instruments for his service?

Am I renewing this dedication day by day and implementing my committal of myself to Christ, in practical outworking?

Am I obeying the command to go on being filled with the Holy Spirit?

ASTER'S STORY
BY COLIN SPENCE

Aster is a gentle, quiet gracious, Eritrean sister in Christ If you were to pass her in the street there would be nothing outwardly about her that would mark her out as being special. But Aster is remarkable, her story is remarkable and she is one of God's 'jewels'. Aster is a prisoner of faith.

Let me tell you just a little of her story…

There was a lot of joy the day that Aster's mother gave birth to her and her identical twin sister. It was something incredible and very special. As the girls grew up they shared many of life's experiences together including coming to faith in Christ. The girls were extremely close and could never have imagined ever being separated from one another. They did everything together.

In July 2008 both women were guests at a wedding type celebration in Eritrea when the security police arrested the wedding party including the guests. They were taken by force, loaded onto trucks and driven to a government 'safe house' that was being used as a detention centre. For four days they were given nothing to eat and interrogated; some of those arrested were released, but not Aster or her twin who steadfastly refused to give up their faith and sign a piece of paper to that effect. That resolute defiance, that commitment to following Christ meant that Aster, her sister and others who refused to sign were taken to prison. In Adi abeto, then Sawa and eventually Wi'a, Aster and her sister were constantly beaten and brutally tortured. In Sawa they were kept imprisoned in shipping containers, in Wia where the heat from the sun is intense and relentless the beatings from the guards was equally intense and relentless. On many occasions the women were singled out for unimaginable suffering and beatings. Made to lie for hours on the burning hot desert stones and then forced into underground cells left to nurse open infected blisters and wounds; little or no food, no medical treatment and no compassion. But always the opportunity and the temptation to deny their faith; sign the paper and secure their release.

Then one evening in the dark of the night, Aster, her sister and another women prisoner were taken from their underground cell out into the bush. They knew exactly what was going to happen to them, they knew they were once again going to be subjected to blow after cruel blow from men that seemed unable to contain their fury almost as if they were possessed. As they reached the spot where the beating was going to take place the women were separated from each other and the guards peeled off to begin their 'work'. 'Those beatings are not meant to kill you', says Aster, 'if you die then you no longer feel pain and they want to inflict as much pain on you as they can'. Aster knew that her Lord had suffered unimaginable pain and that his mother had been a witness to his suffering and death but somehow she never ever imagined being separated from her beloved twin. She never thought for a moment that her sister might die as a result of those beatings, even though she could hear her sister's screams. But that is what happened. Aster and her sister remained faithful and the price for following Christ was the unimaginable. As a result of the beating that night Aster's identical twin went to be with Christ. For weeks Aster believed her sister was in a hospital or a clinic somewhere, recovering. The guards never admitted or told Aster that her sister had died as a result of her injuries. The last experience that the twins shared in this life was when Aster witnessed her sister being beaten to death.

TESTIMONIALS

"Unlike the windowless shipping containers used to torture Christian prisoners in Eretria Dr Berhane Asmelash has provided insight into the suffering and resilience of believers in the little spoken of Eretria, a nation suffering from one of the most repressive regimes in the world today. There are 350 prisons in Eritrea and close to 50,000 prisoners. Most are in prison for reasons of faith and conscience. Many would view a prison cell as a luxury, a hand-dug hole in the ground is home for our brothers and sisters.

Grace flows from every page. The author was fed the mythology that if you want to learn to hate then go to prison. His experience was the very opposite, love flourished in the most inhumane conditions. Of course, we are reminded that love is not a feeling but a choice. The reader will find page after page of descriptions of the most cruel torture, meted out by a philosophy that has abandoned any thought of God. It is said that hell is where God is not found, although the conditions in the Eritrean prisons are truly hellish the beauty of Christ is displayed in the character of his people and the power of the gospel to convert.

We are humbled by the Eritrean experience as the Church in the west is reminded that the issues which divide us are inconsequential. Persecution brings unity. The presence of a gun pressed to the head focuses the soul on what is important. The prayerful influence of the western church is also recognised as it provides an antidote to the unremitting Godless propaganda which tells the prisoner of faith that they are worthless. We are reminded that the knowledge that the whole world is remembering them and praying for them changes everything.

As you hear the story of Dr Berhane, a man who renounced freedom for prison and a lucrative career for ministry you will be humbled and inspired. You will also hear of Merhawi, Timotewos, Twen and many others who refused to be released or freed in order to gain an even better freedom and resurrection.

This book will stir your heart, your tears, your prayers and even your anger which we pray will be as righteous as that of the martyrs of the Church in Eritrea."

Revd David Meredith,
Mission Director, Free Church of Scotland

"This is an amazing book that brings the reader a little closer to the understanding of life for a Christian in Eritrea. I appreciate the historical background of Ethiopia and Eritrea that lays the foundation for understanding the challenge of living in a country of so much conflict. This along with the strong influence of the established Orthodox church and large Muslim faith community hostile to evangelical Christianity. Then to read of Dr Berhane's family heritage of faith in Jesus Christ that enabled them to overcome poverty and opposition and his personal journey to make this faith his own. To read of his intense persecution but also prolific evangelical ministry is both inspiring and salutary as it reminds of our responsibility of being in the 'One Body' of Jesus Christ world-wide. [Berhane's life story] enables him to be an authentic voice for those in his country of Eritrea who are suffering persecution, imprisonment and torture for their faith in Jesus Christ.

I would recommend this book to anyone who wants to read of the life of Jesus Christ in His followers today. It will lead them to the person of Jesus and His power to enable to overcome, whatever the situation. The reader is left challenged and inspired to pray, support and provide for our brothers and sisters who suffer for sharing the Gospel and to join with Dr Berhane in being a voice in seeking justice in their situations."

Mrs Margaret Evans,
Crofton Lane Baptist Church, Release International volunteer.

COLIN SPENCE

This book is also dedicated to Colin Spence who was called home to the Lord in 2019. He was the Release International Prisoners of Faith Manager working in many countries, including Eritrea. He is survived by his wife Winnie, and sons Gareth, Evan, and Ryan. At his funeral in Belfast, many Eritreans celebrated Colin's tireless service to their cause. We are forever grateful for Colin's discreet ministry of selfless compassion to thousands of prisoners of faith. Risen in Glory.

"'Blessed are the dead who die in the Lord from now on.' 'Yes,' says the Spirit, 'they will rest from their labour, for their deeds will follow them.'"

Revelation 14:13